Prayers for Children

Prayers for Children

Compiled by
Christopher Herbert

North American Edition

Forward Movement Publications
Cincinnati, Ohio

This book is dedicated in gratitude to Dorothy Herbert and Eric Turner, in loving memory of Walter Herbert and Gladys Turner.

ISBN 0 88028 149 9
Order no. 1247

First published in 1993 by
The National Society and Church House Publishing

Introduction and compilation © 1993
The Historical Society (Church of England)
for Promoting Religious Education
North American edition, 1994,
Forward Movement Publications,
412 Sycamore Street,
Cincinnati, Ohio 45202-4195 USA
by permission of the original publisher.

Cover illustration: *Portrait of a Child* by Augustus John, reproduced by kind permission of the members of the Junior Common Room, Exeter College, Oxford

Text design by Sarah Smith
Cover design by Leigh Hurlock

Contents

Introduction

An open letter to those who pray with children

I shall have to begin with a story. It concerns my father, a strong and stocky man with pale blue eyes, grey hair and a weather-beaten face. I was sitting next to him one day in a church when I was a small child; as was his custom when he went into a church, he knelt to pray. And it was the very fact of this strong man going down on his knees in such a humble fashion that taught me the importance of prayer.

I had, of course, received instruction from my Sunday School teacher (a lady of advancing years with a broad smile and a grey felt hat); and I knew in my day school that "hands together, and eyes closed" was the proper posture, though through half-opened eyes I squinted to see whether the teachers prayed like the rest of us. Many didn't. I had also been encouraged by my mother and by one of my aunts, but somehow all I could understand was that prayer was important, not overly-important, not self-consciously important, just plain important, like water or bread or the wind in the trees. And ever since then I have continued to pray, because my prayers had the feeling that they were being heard, listened to by God. It was a remarkably special kind of conversation, filled with silence, an awareness of cold knees on a cold, linoleum floor, and yet also touched with the intense and sweet joy of heaven.

How do children learn to pray?

The answers are simple: by observation; by learning from adults; by trying out words for themselves; by trying the lilting words of others. But most important of all, by being allowed to discover that God is and, what is more, that in God's sight they matter tremendously. They are so special to God that they are his children, loved without limit.

Out of that relationship of trust and love, prayer may grow, slowly, hesitantly, with repetition, with humour, with honesty. And as that relationship grows, so the prayers used will change and develop. "God bless Mummy and Daddy" is authentic but needs to be enlarged as the child grows, so that the joys and problems encountered as they grow up can also find their place in prayer. But if you are hesitant in saying prayers with your children — no matter. Reticence is a proper part of prayer, but between you, as you talk with your child and your child talks with you, you will develop a pattern of prayer appropriate for yourself and your child.

Stages in prayer

You may have noticed that the world has gone measurement mad. Everything our children do is measured: their height, their weight, their abilities at school. And there is a great temptation to want to measure spiritual progress as well. Heaven forbid. The essence of our relationship with God is that it is enfolded in mystery. It is holy, sacred, profound, glorious, beyond comprehension — and certainly beyond measurement. But without wishing to succumb to the desire to measure, we ought to check from time to time whether the prayers we use are appropriate. It is important for children to have the security of routine but also important that some prayers are at the edge of their comprehension. Please do not misunderstand this. Simple prayer simply offered is a blessing, but just as adults can grow in their understanding of God, so can children, and we ought to offer them the means, through prayer, whereby that can happen.

A mixture of the child's own prayers and the prayers of others can be good.

How can we encourage children in prayer?

First of all by taking prayer seriously ourselves. Children soon sense if they are being made to do something which the adult no longer values. It will be as we as adults continue to pray, that we can most be of help to our children.

But it is important to grasp that praying with children is not just home-based. It is also a communal activity: at church, at school or wherever.

The context of prayer is significant. If you are helping children to pray in a church setting, then again the attitudes of the adults in the church will set the agenda. If the adults don't pray, the children won't learn. If the adults pray, the children are bound to pick up the significance.

And if the context of prayer is a school, then the underlying set of values of the school will colour the integrity, or otherwise, of prayer. A school where sarcasm is the characteristic mode of address between teacher and child is not exactly conducive to growth in spirituality. But where a school genuinely values things of the spirit (in music, art, science, literature, the environment) and where a school genuinely values and respects the inner world of the child, then spiritual growth can take place.

And what kinds of prayers?

It is a commonly accepted notion that prayer consists of a variety of expressions: adoration; confession; supplication; self-offering; not to mention thanksgiving and silence. If we are to help children pray then we need to ensure that they are aware of the variety of prayers under these headings, not as a matter of mechanical repetition, not as technique, but as a means of offering them forms of words for the feelings they have but cannot find the means to express. Some of the prayers will need to be in their own words; that's a bit like a staircase where you have to use your own energy to get from the bottom to the top. Some of the prayers will need to be in the words of others; they are like an escalator carrying you upwards.

Problems in prayer

There is no doubt that there are also problems in prayer and for children the over-riding one is unanswered prayer. They are bound to have a view of prayer which is quasi-magical i.e. if you ask for something using the right formula you are bound to get it. But the fact of the matter is that prayer is not like that. There will be times when the request is for the wrong reasons; times when having no answer is a kind of answer in itself, and times when no answer is quite baffling.

There is no point in pretending that prayer, especially intercessory prayer, is straightforward. It isn't. It is a mystery. It is a finite human being in relationship with the infinite. But is is also the Christian belief that God is like a father and that we can approach God as a child, filled with trust and faith and expectation. Perhaps the most helpful picture to understand intercessory prayer is that of the four friends carrying the paralysed man towards Jesus. Intercession is like that, a mixture of straightforward desire and persistence and maybe even a bit of ingenuity. And then having carried our concerns to God, as it were on a stretcher, we leave it to Him, knowing He is Love, to respond.

For children, I suspect, prayers of supplication are the most natural, coupled with prayers of thanksgiving. As they grow older they will begin to need to use prayers of confession and those of adoration, though this latter form of prayer is often difficult. How can you manufacture adoration? Answer: it can be done but it is not satisfactory. Adoration grows out of a deep awareness of the mysterious strength and power and generosity of God, and that awareness is a life-time in the making. Even so, those occasional outbursts of love in childhood when the whole world is flooded with delight and purpose are moments of adoration in themselves.

And then there is silence: lots of it. There is no need for babbling all of the time; no need to make prayer a seamless web of words; there must be time for silence. To be able to assist children in entering silence is a gift. Begin with a very short period of silence, and only gradually extend it until that process of "centring down" becomes natural.

As in all other forms of prayer, if the adults at home or church or school are not willing to pray in silence, the children will find it difficult to learn.

Opportunities in prayer

Whilst there may be problems in prayer, we ought not to get bogged down in them; there are also wonderful new worlds waiting to be explored. It is important, or so it seems to me, to offer prayers aloud or in writing. But don't stop there. Help them paint a prayer or take a photograph which is in itself a prayer — of adoration, thanksgiving, supplication. Encourage the use of the senses in worship: of sight and sound and smell. Use prayers which are learnt off-by-heart; use prayers which have stood the test of time; use prayers which are fresh and new. There is no single prayer (unless it's the Lord's Prayer) which can convey the whole truth of the relationship between God and ourselves; and just as our ordinary human relationships are built on a mixture of the routine and the exceptional, so should be our relationship with God. It is finding and creating a balance which is true for the child but also true for God, which is our task.

And using this book

I have had the greatest of pleasure in compiling and writing this book. No doubt there are many gaps. No doubt it could be improved — but I have tried to find, and where necessary write, a range of prayers which will meet many of the needs of the child and will also give glory to God. I have deliberately included the darker side of human life, partly because children are aware of it, and partly because many prayer books seem wilfully to avoid it. But if this world is God's world, and if God is love, then nothing of the darkness is beyond the reach of His love and healing.

The book has been designed for use in churches and schools. In the former, individual prayers according to the theme for the service can be chosen; in the latter, the themes under which prayers have been arranged might make a subject for a number of acts of school worship.

So now the book is yours to be used as you wish. I hope that you will find it to be a rich quarry of ideas if you are helping children in prayer; but above all I hope that it might help some children to become aware of the love God has for them, and thereby enable them to grow in their relationships with God and with the rest of humanity — and to discover that although prayer often feels as though we are moving towards God, in truth it is God who comes towards us with wounded hands of blessing.

Our Father, who art in heaven,
hallowed be thy name;
thy kingdom come;
thy will be done;
on earth as it is in heaven.
Give us this day our daily bread.
And forgive us our trespasses,
as we forgive those
who trespass against us.
And lead us not into temptation;
but deliver us from evil.

For thine is the kingdom,
the power, and the glory,
for ever and ever. Amen.

Lord of Creation

Creation

1 In the beginning . . .

In the beginning of creation, when God made heaven and earth, the earth was without form and void, with darkness over the face of the abyss, and a mighty wind that swept over the surface of the waters. God said, "Let there be light', and there was light; and God saw that the light was good, and he separated light from darkness. He called the light day, and the darkness night. So evening came, and morning came, the first day.

God said, "Let there be a vault between the waters, to separate water from water." So God made the vault and separated the water under the vault from the water above it, and so it was; and God called the vault heaven. Evening came, and morning came, a second day.

God said, "Let the waters under heaven be gathered into one place, so that dry land may appear"; and so it was. God called the dry land earth, and the gathering of the waters he called seas; and God saw that it was good. Then God said, "Let the earth produce fresh growth, let there be on the earth plants bearing seed, fruit trees bearing fruit each with seed according to its kind." So it was; the earth yielded fresh growth, plants bearing seed according to their kind and trees bearing fruit each with seed according to its kind; and God saw that it was good. Evening came, and morning came, a third day.

God said, "Let there be lights in the vault of heaven to separate day from night, and let them serve as signs both for festivals and for seasons and years. Let them also shine in the vault of heaven to give light on earth." So it was; God made the two great lights, the greater to govern the day and the lesser to govern the night; and with them he made the stars. God put these lights in the vault of heaven to give light on earth, to govern day and night, and to separate light from darkness; and God saw that it was good. Evening came, and morning came, a fourth day.

God said, "Let the waters teem with countless living creatures, and let birds fly above the earth across the vault of heaven." God then created the great sea-monsters and all living creatures that move and swarm in the waters according to their kind, and every kind of bird; and God saw that it was good. So he blessed them and said, "Be fruitful and increase, fill the waters of the seas; and let the birds increase on land." Evening came, and morning came, a fifth day.

God said, "Let the earth bring forth living creatures, according to their kind: cattle, reptiles and wild animals, all according to their kind." So it was; God made wild animals, cattle and all reptiles, each according to its kind; and he saw that it was good. Then God said, "Let us make man in our image and likeness to rule the fish in the sea, the birds of heaven, the cattle, all wild animals on earth and all reptiles that crawl upon the earth." So God created man in his own image; in the image of God he created him; male and female he created them. God blessed them and said to them, "Be fruitful and increase, fill the earth and subdue it, rule over the fish in the sea, the birds of heaven and every living thing that moves upon the earth." God also said, "I give you all plants that bear seed everywhere on earth, and every tree bearing fruit which yields seed: they shall be yours for food.

All green plants I give for food to the wild animals, to all the birds of heaven, and to all reptiles on earth, every living creature." So it was; and God saw all that he had made, and it was very good. Evening came, and morning came, a sixth day.

Thus heaven and earth were completed with all their mighty throng. On the sixth day God completed all the work he had been doing, and on the seventh day he ceased from all his work. God blessed the seventh day and made it holy, because on that day he ceased from all the work he had set himself to do.

This is the story of the making of heaven and earth when they were created.

Genesis 1: 2.1-4 (NEB)

2 *Beautiful world*

Father, you have made the world very beautiful.
Teach us to love our world
and to treat it with reverence and with care,
for Jesus' sake.

3 *Thanks for creation*

Almighty God, King of the Universe,
open our eyes to the glory of your creation,
to the planets and stars,
the seas and the sky,
and give us thankful hearts,
through Jesus Christ our Lord.

4 *Teach me to praise thee*

O God, great and wonderful,
who has created the heavens,
dwelling in the light and beauty thereof;
who has made the earth,
revealing thyself in every flower that opens;
let not mine eyes be blind to thee,
neither let mine heart be dead,
but teach me to praise thee,
even as the lark which offereth her song at daybreak.

St Isidore of Seville (560-636)

5 *God in everything*

God, you are our father and our mother,
the life in all that exists;
thank you for the gift of your wonderful world;
for the gift of ourselves —
and for all whom we love.

6 *A Litany of thanks*

For flowers that bloom about our feet,
Father, we thank thee.
For tender grass so fresh, so sweet,
Father, we thank thee.
For song of bird and hum of bee,
for all things fair we hear or see,
Father in heaven, we thank thee.

For blue of stream and blue of sky,
Father, we thank thee.
For pleasant shade of branches high
Father, we thank thee.
For fragrant air and cooling breeze,
for the beauty of the blooming trees,
Father in heaven, we thank thee.

For this new morning with its light,
Father, we thank thee.
For rest and shelter of the night,
Father, we thank thee.
For health and food, for love and friends,
for everything thy goodness sends,
Father in heaven, we thank thee.

Ralph Waldo Emerson (1803-82)

7 *Praise the Lord*

Praise the Lord from heaven,
you that live in the heights above.
Praise him, all his angels,
all his heavenly armies.

Praise him, sun and moon;
praise him, shining stars.
Praise him, highest heavens,
and the waters above the sky.

Let them all praise the name of the Lord!
He commanded, and they were created;
by his command they were fixed in
their places for ever,
and they cannot disobey.

Praise the Lord from the earth,
sea-monsters and all ocean depths;
lightning and hail, snow and clouds,
strong winds that obey his command.

Praise him, hills and mountains,
fruit-trees and forests;
all animals, tame and wild,
reptiles and birds.

Praise him, kings and all peoples,
princes and all other rulers;
girls and young men,
old people and children too.

Let them all praise the name of the Lord!
His name is greater than all others;
his glory is above earth and heaven.
He made his nation strong,
so that all his people praise him —
the people of Israel, so dear to him.

Praise the Lord!

Psalm 148 (GNB)

8 *Canticle of the sun*

Be thou praised, my Lord, with all thy creatures,
above all Brother Sun, who gives the day and
lightens us therewith . . .

Be thou praised, my Lord, of Sister Moon and the
stars; in the heaven thou hast formed them, clear
and precious and comely . . .

Be thou praised, my Lord, of our Sister Mother
Earth, which sustains and hath us in rule, and
produces divers fruit with coloured flowers and
herbs . . .

Praise ye and bless my Lord, and give thanks,
and serve him with great humility.

St Francis of Assisi (1182-1226)

9 *Life everlasting*

We go back as far as we can think, O Lord,
back and back and back,
and there you are at the very beginning . . .
We praise you for the beginning of things
and for the promise of life everlasting.

10 *Let there be light*

Let there be light:
the light of the moon,
the light of the stars,
the light of the sun,
light on the waters,
light in the clouds,
light in the mountains,
light on the leaves of the shimmering trees.
Let there be light . . .
And it was good.
"Yes," dear God, to the light.

11 *An astronomer's prayer*

I thank Thee, my Creator and Lord,
that Thou hast given me these joys in Thy creation,
this ecstasy over the works of Thy hands.
I have made known the glory of Thy works to men
as far as my finite spirit was able to comprehend Thy infinity.
If I have said anything wholly unworthy of Thee,
or have aspired after my own glory,
graciously forgive me.
Amen.

Johann Kepler (1571-1630)

12 *Sing praise to God*

It is good to sing praise to our God;
it is pleasant and right to praise him.
The Lord is restoring Jerusalem;
he is bringing back the exiles.
He heals the broken-hearted
and bandages their wounds.

He has decided the number of the stars
and calls each one by name.
Great and mighty is our Lord;
his wisdom cannot be measured.
He raises the humble,
but crushes the wicked to the ground.

Sing hymns of praise to the Lord;
play music on the harp to our God.
He spreads clouds over the sky;
he provides rain for the earth

and makes grass grow on the hills.
He gives animals their food
and feeds the young ravens when they call.

His pleasure is not in strong horses,
nor his delight in brave soldiers;
but he takes pleasure in those who honour him,
in those who trust in his constant love.

Psalm 147. 1-11 (GNB)

Water

13 *The gift of water*

The whole Israelite community left the desert of Sin, moving from one place to another at the command of the Lord. They made camp at Rephidim, but there was no water there to drink. They complained to Moses and said, "Give us water to drink."

Moses answered, "Why are you complaining? Why are you putting the Lord to the test?"

But the people were very thirsty and continued to complain to Moses. They said, "Why did you bring us out of Egypt? To kill us and our children and our livestock with thirst?"

Moses prayed earnestly to the Lord and said, "What can I do with these people? They are almost ready to stone me."

The Lord said to Moses, "Take some of the leaders of Israel with you, and go on ahead of the people. Take along the stick with which you struck the Nile. I will stand before you on a rock at Mount Sinai. Strike the rock, and water will come out of it for the people to drink." Moses did so in the presence of the leaders of Israel.

Exodus 17. 1-6 (GNB)

14 *The refreshment of water*

Father,
water is so clear,
so bright,
so sparkling in the sun;
let my life be like that water,
full of joy and happiness.

15 *Rain for life*

Lord, thank you for the rain
because it makes many plants live.
Lord, thank you for creating the earth
because on it there live so many races.
I'd like so much that everybody prayed,
that everybody asked your forgiveness.
In the name of Christ I ask you.
Amen.

16 *Sea*

Thank you God for happy days,
Christmas, birthdays,
and time for playing with toys.
Thank you God for holidays,
walking on the pier,
playing on the soft warm sand,
and swimming in the bouncing sea.
I like to watch the waves tossing around,
as they remind me of your love all around us.

17 *Energy for life*

The water comes crashing down the mountain,
turning water-wheels, driving turbines,
giving us energy for our work and our play.
Come to us, Lord, like that,
and fill our lives with the energy of your Holy Spirit,
that we may bring life to others.

18 *The pleasure of water*
(to be said, looking at a jug of water)

Father, the water is . . .
We use it for . . .
Thank you, with all our hearts,
for the use and pleasure of water . . .

Mountains and hills

19   *The holy mountain*

The people of Israel left Rephidim, and on the first day of the third month after they had left Egypt they came to the desert of Sinai. There they set up camp at the foot of Mount Sinai, and Moses went up the mountain to meet with God.

The Lord called to him from the mountain and told him to say to the Israelites, Jacob's descendants: "You saw what I, the Lord, did to the Egyptians and how I carried you as an eagle carries her young on her wings and brought you here to me. Now, if you will obey me and keep my covenant, you will be my own people. The whole earth is mine, but you will be my chosen people, a people dedicated to me alone, and you will serve me as priests." So Moses went down and called the leaders of the people together and told them everything that the Lord had commanded him. Then all the people answered together, "We will do everything that the Lord has said," and Moses reported this to the Lord.

The Lord said to Moses, "I will come to you in a thick cloud, so that the people will hear me speaking with you and will believe you from now on."

Moses told the Lord what the people had answered, and the Lord said to him, "Go to the people and tell them to spend today and tomorrow purifying themselves for worship. They must wash their clothes and be ready the day

after tomorrow. On that day I will come down on Mount
Sinai where all the people can see me. Mark a boundary
round the mountain that the people must not cross, and tell
them not to go up the mountain or even get near it. If anyone
sets foot on it, he is to be put to death."

Exodus 19. 1-12 (GNB)

20   *On top of a mountain*

Lord, I climbed up a huge mountain
and from the top I could look down on the birds,
look down on the trees
and look down on the villages far away.
I had never been so high up before.
Thank you for letting me see your world
in a new and lovely way.

21   *The stillness of mountains*

Mountains are very still,
they just sit and sit.
They point to your greatness, O God,
silent and quiet.
Help me to be still and silent,
Like a mountain.
Sitting still, listening to your voice.

Timothy King

22 *Climbing a rock*

Lord, I saw a man climbing up a steep rock
and I felt frightened.
When things happen to me that are a bit like climbing rocks,
help me to remember that you are always with me
protecting and guiding me with your love.

23 *Skiing*

Thank you, God, for the snow on the mountains —
for skis and toboggans,
for bright warm clothes
and the wind blowing on my face.
Thank you for all the gifts you have given us
and help us to enjoy them to the full —
our Creator and most loving Lord.

Oceans, seas and rivers

24 *Storm on a lake*

One day Jesus got into a boat with his disciples and said to
them, "Let us go across to the other side of the lake." so they
started out. As they were sailing, Jesus fell asleep. Suddenly
a strong wind blew down on the lake, and the boat began to
fill with water, so that they were all in great danger. The disciples went to Jesus and woke him up, saying, "Master,
Master! We are about to die!"

Jesus got up and gave an order to the wind and the
stormy water; they died down, and there was a great calm.
Then he said to the disciples, "Where is your faith?"

But they were amazed and afraid, and said to one
another, "Who is this man? He gives orders to the winds and
waves, and they obey him!"

Luke 8. 22-25 (GNB)

25 *Blessing of the sea*

Lord,
I sing your praise,
The whole day through until the night.
Dad's nets are filled;
I have helped him.

We have drawn them in,
stamping the rhythm with our feet,
the muscles tense.
We have sung your praise.
On the beach, there were our mammies,
who brought the blessing out of the nets,
out of the nets into their baskets.
They rushed to the market,
returned and brought again.
Lord, what a blessing is the sea
with fish in plenty.
Lord, that is the story of your grace.
Lord, with your praise we drop off to sleep.
Carry us through the night;
make us fresh for the morning.
Hallelujah for the day!
and blessing for the night!

A Ghanaian fisherman's prayer

26 Lifeboatmen

Thank you, heavenly Father, for those who risk their lives
in storms and great dangers
to bring others to safety;
when they are frightened, protect them;
when they are in peril, comfort them
and give them at all times,
your peace and your strength, for Jesus' sake.

27 *Merchant and Royal Navies*

Father, when Jesus lived in Palestine,
he brought peace to the storm on the lake.
May he also bring his peace
to those who spend their lives on the oceans of the world,
that they may be aware of his presence every day.

28 *For the river*

Protect, O Lord, we beseech thee,
all those who fish in the rivers and creeks of this country.
Give strength to their arms
as they paddle their canoes and cast their nets.
Grant them success in their work.
In the anxious hours of waiting,
steady and support them,
and grant them in dangers often,
in watching often, in weariness often,
they may have a quiet mind;
through Jesus Christ our Lord.

29 *Rock and sand*

The sea sweeps up the beach
and laps around the sandcastles
until they crumble and fall.
On the farther side of the beach
the sea dashes against the rocks
and they stand firm and strong.
Make us more like rock than sand, Lord.

30 *Those at sea*

Almighty and eternal God, whose way is on the deep,
We commend to thy fatherly care all
that go down to the sea in ships
and occupy their business in great waters.
Help them in whatever lies before them,
to acquit themselves like men.
If there be any duty, may they do it
with cheerfulness.
If any danger, may they face it
with courage,
knowing thy hand is in all things
and all things are in thy hand.
We ask it for thy Name's sake.

31 *Fish-harvest*

Plaice, mackerel, haddock and cod,
these are the fish we eat, O God.
For prawns and shrimps, sardines on toast,
praise Father, Son and Holy Ghost.

32 *The builders of boats*

Lord God bless the people who build the boats.
May they be skilful in all that they do,
true in their craft,
and beautiful in their design,
for Jesus' sake.

Colours

33 A rainbow story

God said to Noah and his sons, "I am now making my covenant with you and with your descendants, and with all living beings — all birds and all animals — everything that came out of the boat with you. With these words I make my covenant with you: I promise that never again will all living things be destroyed by a flood; never again will a flood destroy the earth. As a sign of this everlasting covenant which I am making with you and with all living beings, I am putting my bow in the clouds. It will be the sign of my covenant with the world. Whenever I cover the sky with clouds and the rainbow appears, I will remember my promise to you and to all the animals that a flood will never again destroy all living beings. When the rainbow appears in the clouds, I will see it and remember the everlasting covenant between me and all living beings on earth. That is the sign of the promise which I am making to all living beings."

Genesis 9. 8-17 (GNB)

34 *Red*

Lord, when I think of red I think of:
fire-engines . . .
flames . . .
traffic lights . . .
. . . when I am angry, I get red;
I get red in the face,
red in the nose,
red inside.
So please help me to use my anger
to make the world a better place
and hurt neither others nor
myself.

35 *Green*

Lord, when I think of green I think of:
grass . . .
trees . . .
Thank you for all the green and lovely things
that delight our eyes, and give peace to our souls.

36 *Looking at colours*

Thank you Lord for all the rainbows of the world —
the rainbows in flowers
the rainbows in streets
the rainbows in traffic
the rainbows in faces.
We praise and bless you for a rainbow-full world.

37   *A splash of colour*

O Lord, save me from being a dull,
grey person and let the colours of
your creation pattern my life with
your beauty.

38   *A fanfare of colours*

Thank you, God, for artists;
may they work with honesty and love
and reveal to us the hidden beauties
of your world.

Patterns

39 *A pattern for living*

When he saw the crowds he went up the hill. There he took
his seat, and when his disciples had gathered round him he
began to address them. And this is the teaching he gave:

"How blest are those who know their need of God;
the kingdom of heaven is theirs.
How blest are the sorrowful;
they shall find consolation.
How blest are those of a gentle spirit;
they shall have the earth for their possession.
How blest are those who hunger and thirst to see right prevail;
they shall be satisfied.
How blest are those who show mercy;
mercy shall be shown to them.
How blest are those whose hearts are pure;
they shall see God.
How blest are the peacemakers;
God shall call them his sons.
How blest are those who have suffered persecution
for the cause of right;
the kingdom of Heaven is theirs.

Matthew 5. 1-10 (NEB)

40 *Cobwebs*

Today we saw cobwebs glistening in the early sunlight.
We praise you, O God, for the patterns of the world.
They are lovely. Thank you.

41 *Shadows*

When light and dark go together, Lord,
they make changing patterns for us to look at;
keep us aware of the way the world is made
that we may rejoice in its simplicity.

42 *Finding patterns*

These are the patterns we have found:
lichen on a stone, words on paper . . .
Pattern our lives with your colours of love, dear God,
that we may be beautiful for you.

43 *Pattern of the day*

May we accept this day at your hand, O Lord,
as a gift to be treasured,
a life to be enjoyed,
a trust to be kept,
and a hope to be fulfilled;
and all for your glory.

Stanley Pritchard

44 *Pattern of life*

Through every minute of this day,
be with me, Lord!
Through every day of all this week,
be with me, Lord!
Through every week of all this year,
be with me, Lord!
Through all the years of all this life,
be with me, Lord!
So shall the days and weeks and years
be threaded on a golden cord.
And all draw on with sweet accord
unto thy fullness, Lord,
that so, when time is past,
by grace I may at last,
be with thee, Lord.

John Oxenham (1853-1941)

45 *Pattern of God's presence*

When I wake up in the morning,
thank you, God, for being there.
When I come to school each day,
thank you, God, for being there.
When I am playing with my friends,
thank you, God, for being there.
And when I go to bed at night,
thank you, God, for being there.

People

46 *The making of the world and people*

When the Lord God make the universe, there were no plants on the earth and no seeds had sprouted, because he had not sent any rain, and there was no one to cultivate the land; but water would come up from beneath the surface and water the ground.

Then the Lord God took some soil from the ground and formed a man out of it; he breathed life-giving breath into his nostrils and the man began to live.

Then the Lord God planted a garden in Eden, in the East, and there he put the man he had formed. He made all kinds of beautiful trees grow there and produce good fruit. In the middle of the garden stood the tree that gives life and the tree that gives knowledge of what is good and what is bad.

A stream flowed in Eden and watered the garden; beyond Eden it divided into four rivers. The first river is the Pishon; it flows round the country of Havilah. (Pure gold is found there and also rare perfume and precious stones.) The second river is the Gihon; it flows round the country of Cush. The third river is the Tigris, which flows east of Assyria, and the fourth river is the Euphrates.

Then the Lord God placed the man in the Garden of Eden to cultivate it and guard it. He said to him, "You may eat the fruit of any tree in the garden, except the tree that gives knowledge of what is good and what is bad. You must not eat the fruit of that tree; if you do, you will die the same day."

Then the Lord God said, "It is not good for the man to live alone. I will make a suitable companion to help him." So he took some soil from the ground and formed all the animals and all the birds. Then he brought them to the man to see what he would name them; and that is how they all got their names. so the man named all the birds and all the animals; but not one of them was a suitable companion to help him.

Then the Lord God made the man fall into a deep sleep, and while he was sleeping, he took out one of the man's ribs and closed up the flesh. He formed a woman out of the rib and brought her to him. Then the man said,

"At last, here is one of my own kind —

Bone taken from my bone, and flesh from my flesh.

"Woman" is her name because she was taken out of man."

That is why a man leaves his father and mother and is united with his wife, and they become one.

The man and the woman were both naked, but they were not embarrassed.

Genesis 2. 5-25 (GNB)

47 *And God created us in his own image*

God you have given us many of your gifts:
the gift of beauty;
the gift of wonder;
the gift of creation;
the gift of life itself.
Thank you for sharing so much of yourself with us;
may we share ourselves with you.

48 *Creator of Light*

O God, Creator of Light;
at the rising of your sun this morning,
let the greatest of all lights,
your love,
rise like the sun within our hearts.
Prayer of the Armenian Apostolic Church

Animals

49 *A hymn of praise*

All your creatures, Lord, will praise you,
and all your people will give you thanks.
They will speak of the glory of your royal power
and tell of your might,
so that everyone will know your mighty deeds
and the glorious majesty of your kingdom.
Your rule is eternal,
and you are king for ever.
The Lord is faithful to his promises,
and he is merciful in all his acts.
He helps those who are in trouble;
he lifts those who have fallen.
All living things look hopefully to you,
and you give them food when they need it.
You give them enough and satisfy the needs of all.

Psalm 145. 10-16 (GNB)

50 *Pets*

Father, thank you for our pets.
We love our dogs, our cats, our gerbils . . .
Thank you that they give us so much fun.
May we look after them wisely
for you have entrusted them to us.

51 *Cats*

Our cats are called Tigger, Tom and . . .
We love it when they purr; when they stretch;
Thank you, God,
for the grace and the beauty and the mystery of cats.

52 *Dogs*

Our dogs are called . . .
We love it when they play;
when they romp;
when they wag their tails.
Thank you, God, for the huggy friendship of our dogs.

53 *Hamsters*

Our hamsters are called Wobble and . . .
We love it when they wobble their noses
and run on their wheels.
Thank you, God,
for the mischief and fun of our hamsters.

54 *Fish*

Lord, just as our fish rest gently in the water,
may we rest gently on your unending love.

55 *Blessing on animals*

Dear Father, hear and bless
thy beasts and singing birds,
and guard with tenderness
small things that have no words.

56 *God as creator*

He prayeth best who loveth best
all things both great and small,
for the dear God who loveth us
he made and loveth all.

S.T. Coleridge

57 *A safari park*

For the gentleness of giraffes,
we thank you Lord.
For the mischief of monkeys,
we thank you Lord.
For the babble of baboons,
we thank you Lord.
For the equanimity of elephants,
we thank you Lord.

58 *Dolphins*

Thank you, Lord, for dolphins
that dance and dart through the water.
Help us to understand and care for them
so that our world remains a treasure-house of beauty.

59 *Hedgehogs*

The hedgehogs
come snuffling and scuffling
through the garden
like old men walking along a path.
Lord, thank you for the strangeness of hedgehogs.

60 *Lions and tigers, snakes and bees*

We can roar like lions   (roar)
We can growl like tigers   (growl)
We can hiss like snakes   (hiss)
We can buzz like bees   (buzz)
We can be as still and
as quiet as mice;   (silence)
Thank you God for the sounds of your world.

61 *I don't like*

I don't like toads, spiders, rats or snakes.
Sorry, Lord, but there it is . . .
There are times when I don't
understand your creation.

The ugly things,
the weird things,
they puzzle me.
Why did you create them?
Fun?
Despair?
Mistake?
I'm baffled . . .

62 *A "pleasure" of butterflies*

Lord,
you have given to each of your creatures a particular beauty.
Thank you for the silk-soft joy of butterflies.

63 *Transformation*

God,
as the larva is transformed to a butterfly,
so transform our lives
with the resurrection splendour of Jesus Christ.

64 *The tortoise*

Lord, may we wear the armour of faith
and like the tortoise take pains about all we do,
learning that if we live slowly
we may the more appreciate your world.

65 *The cat*

Lord, thank you for the beauty of cats;
may we learn from them
the skill of exploring the world
with all our senses alert.

66 *The elephant*

Lord, thank you for the power and splendour of elephants;
may we learn from them
that power and delicacy can work together for good.

67 *For all animals*

Animals in zoos, in films, in books;
      hundreds, thousands, with different looks:
the monkey and the kangaroo,
the eagle and the cockatoo;
the tall giraffe, the crawling snail,
the tiny mouse, the giant whale;
the bear, the emu and the gnat,
the crab, the donkey and the bat.
Thank you for them, large and small;
thank you, God, who made them all.

68 *Caring for animals*

Hear our humble prayer, O God,
for our friends the animals.
We entreat for them all thy mercy and pity,
and for those who deal with them

50

we ask a heart of compassion, gentle hands and kindly words.
Make us ourselves to be true friends to animals
and so to share the blessing of the merciful.
For the sake of thy son,
the tender-hearted Jesus Christ our Lord.

69 *A prayer for little things*

Dear God,
I bring to you
all the little things on earth:
a feather,
a daisy,
a marble,
a ladybird . . .
They are all your special treasures,
as we are your special treasures.
May we all be beautiful for you
each in our own way,
giving thanks for your infinite care
of even the tiniest things.

70 *A prayer for little ducks*

Dear God,
give us a flood of water.
Let it rain tomorrow and always.
Give us plenty of little slugs
and other luscious things to eat.
Protect all folk who quack
and everyone who knows how to swim.
                    Carmen Bernos de Gasztold

51

71 *The prayer of the tortoise*

A little patience,
O God,
I am coming.
One must take nature as she is!
It was not I who made her!
I do not mean to criticise;
this house is on my back —
it has its points —
but you must admit, Lord,
it is heavy to carry!
Still,
let us hope that this double enclosure,
my shell and my heart,
will never be quite shut to you.

Carmen Bernos de Gasztold

72 *Prayer for a sick animal*

Dear Father God,
My pet is sick and I am sad.
Please make her better and comfort her if she's in pain.
She can't tell me what she's feeling,
but help her to know that I care
and will look after her
and help her all I can,
just as I'm looked after when I'm ill.
Please bless her
and give her the strength she needs to recover.

73 *For animals who suffer*

Heavenly Father,
we pray for all animals
that are unloved or badly treated;
for those that are overworked and underfed;
for those in captivity behind bars;
for those that are hunted;
for those that are in pain;
for those that have to be put down.
Help us, O Lord, to care for all the animals of your creation.

74 *A miscellany of animals*

O God, I thank thee
for all the creatures thou hast made,
so perfect in their kind —
great animals like the elephant and the rhinoceros,
humorous animals like the camel and the monkey,
friendly ones like the dog and the cat,
working ones like the horse and the ox,
timid ones like the squirrel and the rabbit,
majestic ones like the lion and the tiger,
for birds with their songs.
O Lord, give us such love for thy creation
that love may cast out fear,
and all thy creatures see in man
their priest and friend;
through Jesus Christ our Lord.

George Appleton

Plants and trees

75 *Planted like a tree*

Happy are those who reject the advice of evil men,
who do not follow the example of sinners
or join those who have no use for God.
Instead, they find joy in obeying the Law of the Lord,
and they study it day and night.
They are like trees that grow beside a stream,
that bear fruit at the right time,
and whose leaves do not dry up.
They succeed in everything they do.

But evil men are not like this at all;
they are like straw that the wind blows away.
Sinners will be condemned by God
and kept apart from God's own people.
The righteous are guided and protected by the Lord,
but the evil are on the way to their doom.

Psalm 1 (GNB)

76 *Plant life*

For the softness of moss,
we thank you, O Lord.
For the strength of the oak tree,
we thank you, O Lord.
For the fragrance of roses,
we thank you, O Lord.
For all the plants in all of the world,
we thank you, O Lord.

77 *Acorns and oak trees*

Inside the acorn is a strong and beautiful tree
waiting to spring into life.
Thank you, Lord,
for such a big promise in such a tiny space.

78 *New leaves unfolding*

Almighty God, Creator of this wonderful world,
we rejoice at the signs of new life . . .
May we be *Spring* to others
and never *Winter*.

79 *Protection of the environment*

O holy and loving Father,
you have created for us a wonderful world:
please forgive us when we cause harm
to your creation
and teach us how to love and cherish
everything that has life,
that our world may remain
a place of beauty and boundless glory,
now and for ever.

80 *God loves all that is*

There is not a single person,
not a single bird,
not a single blade of grass
which is outside your love, O Lord;
— for you give life to everything,
and for your humble power,
we give you thanks and praise.

81 *The silhouette of a tree at twilight*

The tree silhouetted against the sky looks like . . .
lace . . .
cobwebs . . .
For the shapes and clean beauty of trees in Autumn,
we thank you, Heavenly Father.

82 *Squirrels*

The squirrels dart here and there,
finding and storing food for the winter.
We thank you, God, for the bright energy of squirrels
and for all that makes our world a place of beauty.

83 *Old age*

Sometimes old people look like old trees,
bent and weary and sad.
We pray for them
that in their hearts they may know your peace and love,
O Lord.

Birds

84 *God: creator of birds*

How fast the wings of an ostrich beat!
But no ostrich can fly like a stork.
The ostrich leaves her eggs on the ground
for the heat in the soil to warm them.
She is unaware that a foot may crush them
or a wild animal break them.
She acts as if the eggs were not hers,
and is unconcerned that her efforts were wasted.
It was I who made her foolish
and did not give her wisdom.
But when she begins to run,
she can laugh at any horse and rider.

Job 39. 13-18 (GNB)

85 *Seagulls*

Like a seagull gliding on the wind
may we trust ourselves to your love, O Lord.

86 *A bird's feather*

Open our eyes, dear Lord,
to the tiny glories of your world,
and accept our thanks as praise.

87 *The skylark*

I couldn't see the skylark —
he was too high up in the sky for that —
but I could hear him.
Music from nowhere, music for the sheer joy of it.
Make us, Lord, as happy as skylarks.

88 *Song-thrush*

When evening is drawing on
and the song-thrush sings,
may I too, O Lord, give thanks to you
with all my heart for the day that is past.

89 *Birds*

Lord, Creator of the eagle and the sparrow,
the dove and the humming bird,
we praise and thank you for the varied beauty
of birds, their songs and their flight.
Help us to care for this marvellous part of your creation;
for your name's sake.

Our Senses

Sight

Jesus and his followers came to Bethsaida. Some people brought a blind man to Jesus and begged him to touch the man. So Jesus took the blind man's hand and led him out of the village. Then he spat on the man's eyes. He put his hands on the blind man and asked, "Can you see now?"

The man looked up and said, "Yes, I see people, but they look like trees walking around."

Again Jesus put his hands on the man's eyes. The man opened his eyes wide. His eyes were healed, and he was able to see everything clearly.

Jesus told him to go home saying, "Don't go into the town."

Jesus and his followers went to the towns around Caesarea Phillipi. While they were travelling, Jesus asked them, "Who do people say I am?"

They answered, "Some people say you are John the Baptist. Others say you are Elijah. And others say that you are one of the prophets.

Then Jesus asked, "Who do you say I am?"

Peter answered, "You are the Christ."

Jesus ordered his followers, "Don't tell anyone who I am."

Mark 8. 22-30 (ICB)

63

91 *Seeing and trusting*

In darkness and in light,
in trouble and in joy,
help us to trust your love,
to serve your purpose,
to praise your name;
through Jesus Christ our Lord.

92 *Doubt*

Dispel, O Lord, O Father of Lights,
all clouds of doubt and the darkness about our earthly course;
that in your light we may see light
and come both to know you as we are known
and to love as we are loved;
through Jesus Christ our Lord.

93 *The eyes of Christ*

Give me courage, God,
to see the world with the eyes of Jesus.

94 *The blind*

Almighty God, Father of all mankind, embrace the blind
with your love,
that they may feel your presence in their inmost souls
and know your guiding hand;
through Jesus Christ our Lord.

95 *Guide dogs*

Bless, O Lord, all those who train guide dogs for the blind.
Enrich their patience and increase their skills
for Jesus' sake.

96 *Eye surgeons*

Give to all eye surgeons, O Lord,
skill, compassion and tenderness,
that all who come into their care
may see your gifts at work in the world.

97 *Sight*

Let us think for a moment
about the wonder of being able to see.
Without sight
we should find it hard to learn anything at all,
and the world would be a sad, dark place.
Thanks be to God our Father for the gift of sight.

Thank you, God, for giving us eyes
to see the world that you have made,
and to learn about it by looking and reading.
May we always see pure and good things
and use our eyesight to your glory,
and in the service of our fellow-men;
through Jesus Christ our Lord.

A.G. Bullivant

98 *For the wonder of sight*

For the wonder of seeing, I praise you,
my Lord and my God.

99 *Medical research*

Almighty God, the Father of truth and understanding;
give a clear vision
to those who are engaged in medical research;
grant them the spirit of patient discernment,
that they may be skilled to find new ways of restoring health;
and encourage them
with the assurance that they are sharing your work;
through Jesus Christ our Lord.

F.B. Macnutt

100 *The blind*

O God, open our eyes to the needs of the blind;
may we treat them with respect and care;
may we be humble enough to learn from them
but above all help us to discover with them
the hidden treasures of our shared humanity.

101 *Eye problems*

God, I am sick.
Heal my right eye.
I cannot see well
and I need to be operated on.
I am afraid
but I know you are near me.
Thank you, God.

Hearing

102 *Helping people hear*

On his return journey from Tyrian territory he went by way
of Sidon to the Sea of Galilee through the territory of the Ten
Towns. They brought to him a man who was deaf and had an
impediment in his speech, with the request that he would
lay his hand on him. He took the man aside, away from the
crowd, put his fingers into his ears, spat, and touched his
tongue. Then, looking up to heaven, he sighed, and said to
him, "Ephphatha", which means "Be opened". With that his
ears were opened, and at the same time the impediment was
removed and he spoke plainly. Jesus forbade him to tell
anyone; but the more he forbade them, the more they
published it. Their astonishment knew no bounds: "all that
he does, he does well," they said; "he even makes the deaf
hear and the dumb speak."

Mark 7. 31-37 (NEB)

103 *The deaf*

Father, I am so glad that I can hear music;
give me sympathy for the deaf
and make me sensitive to their needs.

Bless all who work with them,
all scientists, doctors, social workers, employers and priests
and show me what I can do to help, please . . .

104 *The music of creation*

Blessed Lord, we thank you for the gift of hearing.
Grant that our ears may be open to all loveliness:
to music, and the laughter of our friends;
to running water; to the wind in the trees;
to the call of birds and beasts — and to all the multitude of voices
in your strange creation.

Grant that we may ever hear in them
the music of your love and goodness and power;
through Jesus Christ our Lord.

105 *Hearing*

(Let us be very still for a moment
and think about the wonder of being able to hear.
If we could not hear,
the world would be a dull and silent place.
Thanks be to God our Father
for giving us the sense of hearing.)

Teach us, good Lord, to use our ears to hear good things:
help us to enjoy music, laughter, people talking,
the wind blowing, the birds and animals calling,
and all good things
given to us so freely in this lovely world;
through Jesus Christ our Lord.

A.G. Bullivant

106 *Technology for the deaf*

Dear God, your skill is infinite;
give to all scientists and technicians
the patience and the wisdom, the love and the dedication
to create new ways for deaf people to hear;
so that we all may grow in understanding of you
and of each other.
This we ask for Jesus' sake.

107 *Sign-language*

Thank you, God,
for those who have created new ways of communicating,
so that deaf people may share in our world.
May we be so aware of the needs of the deaf,
that through our lips and our bodies,
through our love and our care,
we may draw close to them and create new understanding;
through Jesus Christ our Lord.

108 *Silence*

Dearest God,
in your compassion
be with those who are deaf;
may their inner ears be open to your Word,
so that in the silences we share
we may discover your beauty
and your most holy love.

Speech

109 *The speech of God*

Before the world was created, the Word already existed; he
was with God, and he was the same as God. From the very
beginning the Word was with God. Through him God made
all things; not one thing in creation was made without him.
The Word was the source of life, and this life brought light to
mankind. The light shines in the darkness, and the darkness
has never put it out.

John 1. 1-5 (GNB)

110 *Saying something helpful*

God grant
that when the chance to say something helpful comes our way,
we shall be brave enough to say it.

111 *Unkind words*

Gracious Lord,
help us to refrain from speaking unkind words,
so that our tongue may be known for its kindness.

112 *Words*

Word of God,
give me the words to praise you
for ever and ever.

113 *Words of Prayer*

When words fail me, Lord,
and I don't know what to make of things,
help me to be really silent, deep-down silent
and wait in trust for the answers.

114 *Speech therapists*

Lord Jesus, Word of God,
you proclaimed your love in story and brought healing
through your speech;
bless all speech therapists
that they may be patient and skilful in their work
and bring to those who suffer
your word of peace and love.

115 *Sounds*

God has given me a voice and a tongue.
I can shout, whisper, sing.
God made the mouth to speak good words.

Teach me, God, to thank and praise,
and with words and deeds
show that I am your child
and want to belong to the kingdom of heaven.

Touch

116 *The sense of touch*

Once Jesus was in a town where a very sick man lived. The man was covered with a harmful skin disease. When he saw Jesus, he bowed before Jesus and begged him, "Lord, heal me. I know you can if you want to."

Jesus said, "I want to. Be healed!" And Jesus touched the man. Immediately the disease disappeared. Then Jesus said, "Don't tell anyone about what happened. But go and show yourself to the priest. And offer a gift to God for your healing as Moses commanded. This will prove to everyone that you are healed."

But the news about Jesus was spreading more and more. Many people came to hear Jesus and to be healed of their sicknesses. But Jesus often slipped away to other places to be alone so that he could pray.

Luke 5. 12-16 (ICB)

117 *Exploring*

O holy God, you have made our world very curious;
help me, as I explore your world,
to be touched by your Presence in everything.

118 *Physiotherapists*

Lord Jesus, you laid your hands on those who were ill
and brought them peace and healing;
pour your healing gifts upon all physiotherapists,
that in word and deed they may bring solace and strength
to all in need.

119 *Holding hands*

In the simple pleasure of holding hands
you have given us, dear Lord, a gentle blessing.
May we always use our hands
to bring peace and joy to those we meet,
so that we may be part of your outpouring love
for us and for all mankind.

120 *Hands who touched the leper*

Hands who touched the leper,
touch my wounded heart;
hands who healed the blind man,
heal my aching soul;
hands who cured the lame,
mend my disjointed life;
hands who embraced all life,
enfold me in your peace.
Lord,
merely touch and heal,
cure and forgive.

Taste

121 *A feast with friends*

Some time later Jesus withdrew to the farther shore of the
Sea of Galilee (or Tiberias), and a large crowd of people
followed who had seen the signs he performed in healing the
sick. Then Jesus went up the hill-side and sat down with his
disciples. It was near the time of Passover, the great Jewish
festival. Raising his eyes and seeing a large crowd coming
towards him, Jesus' said to Philip, "Where are we to buy
bread to feed these people?" This he said to test him; Jesus
himself knew what he meant to do. Philip replied, "Twenty
pounds would not buy enough bread for every one of them
to have a little." One of his disciples, Andrew, the brother of
Simon Peter, said to him, "There is a boy here who has five
barley loaves and two fishes; but what is that among so
many?" Jesus said, "Make the people sit down." There was
plenty of grass there, so the men sat down, about five
thousand of them. Then Jesus took the loaves, gave thanks,
and distributed them to the people as they sat there. He did
the same with the fishes, and they had as much as they
wanted. When everyone had had enough, he said to his
disciples, "Collect the pieces left over, so that nothing may be
lost." This they did, and filled twelve baskets with the pieces
left uneaten of the five barley loaves.

When the people saw the sign Jesus had performed, the

word went round, "Surely this must be the prophet that was
to come in to the world." Jesus, aware that they meant to
come and seize him to proclaim him king, withdrew again to
the hills by himself.

John 6. 1-15 (NEB)

122 *Give us this day our daily bread*

Blessed are you, Lord our God, King of the Universe,
who feeds the entire world in his goodness —
with grace, with kindness and with mercy.
He gives food to all life for his kindness is eternal . . .
Blessed are you, God, who nourishes all.

Jewish Grace

123 *Blessing of food*

The bread is pure and fresh,
the water is cool and clear.
Lord of all life, be with us.
Lord of all life, be near.

African Grace

124 *Thank you for my food*

My God, I thank you for my food.
It is you that allows the rice, the beans, the wheat,
the fruit, the animals and the vegetables to grow.
I thank you for the food that is on the table.
Thank you very much, Lord.

Elizete Simon (aged 11)

125 *The loveliness of things*

Bread is a lovely thing to eat —
God bless the barley and the wheat.
A lovely thing to breathe is air —
God bless the sunshine everywhere.
The earth's a lovely place to know —
God bless the folks that come and go!
Alive's a lovely thing to be —
giver of life — we say — bless thee!

126 *God is great*

God is great,
God is good,
let us thank him for this food.
Amen.

127 *Be present at our table*

Be present at our table, Lord;
be here and everywhere adored.
His mercies bless and grant that we
may strengthened for thy service be.
Amen.

128 *For your love*

For your love; we give you thanks;
For your love; we give you thanks;
For your joy that's like a pearl
Let each boy and every girl
give you thanks,
give you thanks,
give you thanks.

129 *Bless us O Lord*

Bless us, O Lord, and these thy gifts
which of thy bounty we are about to receive;
through Jesus Christ our Lord.
Amen.

130 *For the good of your providing*

Lord God, we thank you
for all the good things of your providing,
and we pray for the time when people everywhere
shall have the abundant life of your will,
revealed to us in Jesus Christ, your Son, our Lord.

George Appleton

Our Feelings

Happiness

131 Being brilliant

"No one lights a lamp and puts it in a cellar, but rather on the lampstand so that those who enter may see the light. The lamp of your body is the eye. When your eyes are sound, you have light for your whole body; but when the eyes are bad, you are in darkness. See to it then that the light you have is not darkness. If you have light for your whole body with no trace of darkness, it will all be as bright as when a lamp flashes its rays upon you."

Luke 11. 33-36 (NEB)

132 Happiness is . . . parents and grandparents

being with Mummy and Daddy . . .
being with Nana and Grandpa . . .

Dear God, we are really happy,
deep-down-comfy-happy when we are with . . .
Please bless them with your love today,
tomorrow and forever.

133 *Happiness is . . . friends*

making a new friend . . .
playing with . . .

We think friends are friends when
— we can play together and not get cross
— we can . . .

These are the names of our friends . . .
We hold them up to you in thanksgiving.

134 *Happiness is . . . "all the b's"*

having a warm bath . . .
hearing a book when we are in bed . . .

For balloons and baths and books and beds,
we bless you, heavenly Father.

135 *Happiness is . . . going to the seaside*

These are the sounds of the sea . . .
— sh, lap, splash, splish,
crash, ripple, hush, roar . . .

For the sun on the sea:	we bless you, Lord.
For the shine of the sea:	we bless you, Lord.
For the splash of the sea:	we bless you, Lord.
For the sparkle of the sea:	we bless you, Lord.
For all the sounds and sights of the seaside:	we bless you, Lord, forever.

136 *Happiness is . . . a theme park*

These are the things we did at the theme park . . .

Lord,
For water-chutes and dashing dodgems: Hooray.
For whizzing planes and great big dippers: Hooray.
For tunnels, mazes, slides and swings: Hooray.
For all that makes us really happy: Hooray, Hooray, Hooray.

137 *God loves me*

God is with me now.
God sees me.
God hears me.
God smiles at me.
God loves me.
God wants me . . .
now and always.
St Saviour's Priory

138 *Happy together*

Thank you, God, that we have come together.
Thank you, God, that we could giggle together.
Thank you, God, that we could eat together.
Thank you, God, that we could see together.
Thank you, God, that we could pray together.

139 *Loving hearts*

O Lord, give us, we beseech thee, in the name of Jesus
Christ,
that love which shall never cease,
that will kindle our lamps but never extinguish them,
that we may enlighten others and may always desire thee.

St Columba

140 *God Bless . . .*

God bless all those that I love;
God bless all those that love me;
God bless all those that love those that I love,
and all those that love those that love me.

From an old New England sampler

141 *Using our gifts*

O God, thank you for the gift of life
and for the faculties which enable us to enjoy it.
You have given us our eyes to see the beauty of the world,
our ears to hear speech and the sound of music,
our lips with which to speak in friendship to others,
and our hands with which to minister to their needs.
Help us, through the grace of your Holy Spirit,
to use all that we have in your service
and for your greater glory;
through Jesus Christ our Lord.

142 *Morning*

Oh, shining morning, when I kneel to pray,
my loathsome, blinded body all forgot,
the door shut,
I together with my thoughts,
alone, amid the loveliness of dawn.

Miyoshi, a Japanese leprosy patient

143 *Thank you God*

We thank thee, God, for the moments of fulfilment:
the end of a hard day's work,
the harvest of sugar cane,
the birth of a child,
for in these pauses,
we feel the rhythm of the eternal.
Amen.

Prayer from Hawaii

Sadness

144 *The raising of Lazarus*

Jesus arrived in Bethany. Then he learned that Lazarus had already been dead in the tomb for four days. Bethany was about three kilometres from Jerusalem. Many Jews had come there to comfort Martha and Mary about their brother.

Martha heard that Jesus was coming, and she went out to meet him. But Mary stayed at home. Martha said to Jesus, "Lord, if you had been here, my brother would not have died. But I know that even now God will give you anything you ask."

Jesus said, "Your brother will rise and live again."

Martha answered, "I know that he will rise and live again in the resurrection on the last day."

Jesus said to her, "I am the resurrection and the life. He who believes in me will have life even if he dies. And he who lives and believes in me will never die. Martha, do you believe this?"

Martha answered, "Yes, Lord. I believe that you are the Christ, the Son of God. You are the One who was coming to the world."

After Martha said this, she went back to her sister Mary. She talked to Mary alone. Martha said, "The Teacher is here and he is asking for you." When Mary heard this, she got up quickly and went to Jesus. Jesus had not yet come into the town. He was still at the place where Martha had met him. The Jews were with Mary in the house, comforting her. They saw Mary stand and leave quickly. They followed her, thinking that she was going to the tomb to cry there. But Mary went to the place where Jesus was. When she saw him, she fell at his feet and said, "Lord, if you had been here, my brother would not have died."

Jesus saw that Mary was crying and that the Jews who came with her were crying, too. Jesus felt very sad in his heart and was deeply troubled. He asked, "Where did you bury him?"

"Come and see, Lord," they said.

Jesus cried.

So the Jews said, "See how much he loved him."

But some of them said, "If Jesus healed the eyes of the blind man, why didn't he keep Lazarus from dying?"

Again Jesus felt very sad in his heart. He came to the tomb. The tomb was a cave with a large stone covering the entrance. Jesus said, "Move the stone away."

Martha said, "But Lord, it has been four days since he died. There will be a bad smell." Martha was the sister of the dead man.

Then Jesus said to her, "Didn't I tell you that if you believed, you would see the glory of God?"

So they moved the stone away from the entrance. Then Jesus looked up and said, "Father, I thank you that you heard me. I know that you always hear me. But I said these things because of the people here around me. I want them to believe that you sent me." After Jesus said this, he cried out in a loud voice, "Lazarus, come out!" The dead man came out. His hands and feet were wrapped with pieces of cloth, and he had a cloth around his face.

John 11. 17-44 (ICB)

145 *Bereavement*

Lord God, Father and creator of us all, thank you for . . .
We feel very sad.
Through our own sadness, help us to
understand the sadness of others
and try to make the world a kinder place.

146 *The death of a grandparent*

Lord in heaven, you have promised us new life
through your Son, Jesus Christ;
help us to live with that promise
in our hearts and in our lives,
so that our sadness can be turned by you
into blessing and strength in the days ahead.

147 *Disasters*

We saw pictures on the television of . . .
Lord God, be the strength
of all those who are in terrible sorrow,
that they may be helped in their despair
and find your light,
even where all seems to be utter darkness.

148 *Suffering*

Dear God, how can we bear the knowledge of hunger,
of babies crying continually,

of children who grow thin and misshapen,
of mothers who give up their own share,
and fathers who face despair?
Forgive those of us who forget,
and teach us to remember.
Cherish those who can never forget,
who wait with Christ in the wilderness.

Monica Furlong

149 *The suffering servant*

Who would have believed what we heard?
Who saw the Lord's power in this?
He grew up like a small plant before the Lord.
He was like a root growing in a dry land.
He had no special beauty or form to make us notice him.
There was nothing in his appearance to make us desire him.
He was hated and rejected by people.
He had much pain and suffering.
People would not even look at him.
He was hated and we didn't even notice him.
But he took our suffering on him and felt our pain for us.

Isaiah 53. 1-4 (ICB)

150 *Violence*

Lord, we hold up to you those people who have been so violent.
We don't want to pretend that we aren't violent at times.
So, Lord, here we are —
puzzled by our fellow men and puzzled by ourselves.
Please make sense of us.

151 *The hungry*

Our prayer, Lord,
is that we shall do something to feed the hungry
and shall work for justice in the world,
through Jesus Christ our Lord.

152 *The poor*

We hold up to you, God, all the poor on the earth;
may we who are rich share our wealth;
we who are well fed share our food;
we who are educated share our learning;
so that in our own small way
we may contribute to the coming of your kingdom.

153 *Racism* (a "rap" prayer)

Loving God and heavenly Father,
you have made us humans very colourful:
— some white, some pink, some black, some brown,
some olive, some dark, some light — a crown
of glory which fits us all,
the short, the thin, the fat, the tall.
So let your blessing be on our world
that human kind with joy unfurled
may learn to live in love and peace
and hatred may for ever cease . . .

154 *War*

Lord God,
let your peace rest so gently on our hearts and minds
that we may have the strength
to work for peace in our world,
today, tomorrow and for ever.

155 *Disasters*

God of goodness and love,
in whom we can trust in every hour of need;
have mercy on all who are faced with fear and distress
(through earthquake, tempest, pestilence, flood . . .).
We ask that help may be given to them speedily,
and that this emergency may be turned into an opportunity
to strengthen the bonds of love and service
which bind men and nations together;
through Jesus Christ our Lord.

Christian Aid

156 *Prisoners*

We pray, our Father,
for those whose freedom has been taken from them:
for all who suffer imprisonment,
whether for crime or for conscience' sake;
for all whose vision of your world is seen through bars,
and in whose heart the lamp of hope burns low.
God of mercy, give them help, according to their need,
and hear our prayer for Jesus Christ's sake.

Timothy Dudley-Smith

157 *Tears*

Almighty God, Father of all mankind,
in your Son you took upon yourself the world's sorrow.
We offer you our own sorrow and sadness
knowing that you can help us to bear our grief
through the infinite understanding and love
of Jesus Christ our Lord.

158 *The surrounding love of God*

Almighty God, who seest that we have no power of
ourselves
to help ourselves;
keep us both outwardly in our bodies
and inwardly in our souls
that we may be defended from all adversities
which may happen to the body and from all evil thoughts
which may assault and hurt the soul;
through Jesus Christ our Lord.

159 *Those in need*

Lord Christ, shine upon all
who are in the darkness of suffering or grief;
that in your light they may receive hope and courage,
and in your presence may find their rest and peace;
for your love's sake.

Alan Warren

160 *The leper*

Men hate me for the curse I bear,
(I know it well),
but shall I heed them
since my heart can be
a holy temple
where my God can dwell?
      Handa, a Japanese leprosy patient

161 *O God we hope in you*

O God, we hope in you
that you will help us in all our troubles;
that you will strengthen us in all our temptations;
that you will forgive us all our sins;
that you will be with us when we die,
and be merciful to us when we are judged.
O God, in you have we trusted; let us never be confounded.

162 *Feeling down*

Lord Jesus,
everything seems to have gone wrong for me today.
I'm feeling very little
and people seem to hurt me so easily.
Thank you for always being there.
Thank you that you care.

163 *Feeling lonely*

Father God,
everyone else seems to have lots of friends except me.
Thank you that when I feel alone I can pray to you.
Deep down I know that I'm not alone
but that you are here beside me.

164 *Our hope and strength*

Lord, you are our hope and strength,
staying with us in trouble,
walking with us in danger,
and comforting us in our sadness.
Keep us always mindful of your love,
that we may be strong and courageous
in all we think and speak and do,
knowing that you are our closest
and our most loyal friend.

Anger, worry and fear

165 *Receiving peace and support*

So a pupil should be satisfied to become like his teacher, and
a slave like his master. If the head of the family is called
Beelzebul, the members of the family will be called even
worse names!

So do not be afraid of people. Whatever is now covered
up will be uncovered, and every secret will be made known.
What I am telling you in the dark you must repeat in broad
daylight, and what you have heard in private you must
announce from the housetops. Do not be afraid of those who
kill the body but cannot kill the soul; rather be afraid of God,
who can destroy both body and soul in hell.

Matthew 10. 25-28 (GNB)

166 *Christ who calms fears . . .*

O Christ, who hast known fear,
be with all who are afraid today.
United Society for the Propagation of the Gospel

167 *A sure refuge*

O God,
who has been the refuge of my fathers
through many generations,
be my refuge today
in every time and circumstance of need.
Be my guide
through all that is dark and doubtful.
Be my guide
against all that threatens my spirit's welfare.
Be my strength
in time of testing.
Gladden my heart with thy peace;
through Jesus Christ my Lord.

John Baillie

168 *Bringing harmony*

God of the green pastures and still waters,
help my heart to beat in time
with the quiet music of your creation.

169 *Alone*

Alone with none but Thee, my God,
I journey on my way.
What need I fear when Thou art near,
O King of night and day?
More safe am I within Thy hand
than if a host did round me stand.

St Columba

170 *Feeling angry*

Sometimes I find it hard, Lord,
to sit and listen to you.
My anger gets in the way,
and my mind criss-crosses
with nasty thoughts.
Help me to share my anger with you
and not to let it swallow me up.
Help me not to make other people angry with me,
but show me how to be loving.

Timothy King

171 *Gentle Jesus, be with us today*

Gentle Jesus,
be with us today.
I ask you, give us all our daily needs.
Gentle Jesus,
I ask you to be with all those in hospitals.
Give them strength to pray to you.
Be with our parents at home.
Jesus, be with us
as we talk to you every day and listen to you.
Be with those who are sad.
Let them know that you are their Father
so they cannot feel alone.
Be with us now and forever.
Amen.

172 *A sense of humour*

Give us a sense of humour, Lord,
and also things to laugh about.
Give us grace to take a joke against ourselves,
and see the funny side of the things we do.
Save us from annoyance, bad temper, resentfulness
against our friends.
Help us to laugh
even in the face of trouble.
Fill our minds with the love of Jesus;
for his name's sake.

A.G. Bullivant

173 *Honest anger*

Dear God,
it's like a flame, my anger.
It begins deep down and roars into life
and I am frightened by its power:
but help me to use that power wisely and for good
where things really are wrong
or where people are being hurt,
so that truth may be honoured,
wounds may be healed
and justice be given room to grow.

Families and Friends

Mothers, fathers and families

174 *Jesus and his family*

When Joseph and Mary had finished doing all that was required by the law of the Lord, they returned to their home town of Nazareth in Galilee. The child grew and became strong; he was full of wisdom, and God's blessings were upon him.

Every year the parents of Jesus went to Jerusalem for the Passover Festival. When Jesus was twelve years old they went to the festival as usual. When the festival was over, they started back home, but the boy Jesus stayed in Jerusalem. His parents did not know this; they thought that he was with the group, so they travelled a whole day and then started looking for him among their relatives and friends. They did not find him so they went back to Jerusalem looking for him. On the third day they found him in the Temple, sitting with the Jewish teachers, listening to them and asking questions. All who heard him were amazed at his intelligent answers. His parents were astonished when they saw him, and his mother said to him, "My son, why have you done this to us? Your father and I have been terribly worried trying to find you."

He answered them, "Why did you have to look for me? Didn't you know that I had to be in my Father's house?" But they did not understand his answer.

So Jesus went back with them to Nazareth, where he was obedient to them. His mother treasured all these things in her heart. Jesus grew both in body and in wisdom, gaining favour with God and men.

Luke 2. 39-52 (GNB)

175   *The prayer of parents*

O God, you have given us a share
in the creation of new life.
When things go well, may we be thankful;
when we are in despair, comfort us;
when we have lost hope, renew our strength;
when we are at peace, cherish us.
And at all times, O God,
fill our hearts with love
for our children, each other and for you.

176   *Parents*

Lord,
I remember my parents,
my brothers and sisters.
My day was easy,
my arms are not swollen,
my back does not hurt.

Lord,
I was sitting on a stool
while father dug in the ground.
I drew the lines on the paper
while mother prepared the meals
and everybody busied himself for me.

Lord,
keep my parents in Your love.
Lord,
bless them and keep them.
Lord,
please let me have money and strength
and keep my parents for many more years
so that I can take care of them.
Prayer of a young Ghanaian Christian

177 *Parents, when anxious*

Direct with your loving kindness our parents, O God.
When they are tired, strengthen them;
when they are worried, sustain them;
when they are bewildered, encourage them;
and in all their fears give them your hope and peace
that their lives may be renewed
today, tomorrow and for ever.

178 *Families*

Bless, O God, our families:
give to those who care for us
the spirit of understanding, the spirit of love;
that our homes may be places of peace and of laughter;
for Jesus' sake.

179 *Brothers and sisters*

Holy Father, heavenly king,
let your blessing rest upon our brothers and sisters
and all our family,
that our lives together may be touched
by the strength and the laughter of heaven.

180 *Homes*

God, make my home a better place
and begin the change with me . . .

181 *When a parent has left home*

I boil with anger
when I think about it . . .
and then at other times I weep . . .
Why? Lord!
Why did my mother/father leave home?
Couldn't they see how I would feel?
Didn't they care?

And when I am in black despair,
confused and frightened by it all,
help me to know that you are with me
and will comfort and strengthen me always . . .
and will bring me into new life
and surround me with your peace.

182 *A prayer for blessing of parents*

Heavenly Father, bless all parents;
give them thankful hearts when things go well
and in the hard times give them loving kindness;
through Jesus Christ our Lord.

183 *Family strife*

Dearest God,
my parents trouble me with their rows and quarrels,
and I hate it when they shout at each other.
I bring this to you, for I need you now more than ever.
God — be my friend.

184 *Family peace*

Visit, we beseech thee, O Lord, our homes
and drive far from them the snares of the enemy:
let thy holy angels dwell therein
to preserve us in peace:
and may thy blessing be upon us evermore;
through Jesus Christ our Lord.

Book of Common Prayer (1928)

185 *Mothers*

Lord, we thank you for our mothers
and the gift of
their tenderness and understanding,
their patience and thoughtfulness,
their kindness and love.

We can be so wilful,
so thoughtless,
so impatient,
and so unkind;
for often we demand without grace
and receive without thanks
and always we expect more.
We expect our mothers to be there
to cater to our selfishness,
and then we wonder why she gets tired
and irritable
and thoroughly fed up.
Yet through all these things she loves us.

Lord, teach us to be thoughtful
and understanding and sensitive to our mother's needs,
that we may ease her days
and increase her joy.
We ask this through the generous and loving example
of our saviour, Jesus Christ. Amen.

Giles Harcourt

186 *Father-and-Mother God*

Dear Father-and-Mother God,
thank you for my mother and father
and for all their love to me.
My mum is so loving and my dad so strong,
I feel safe with them.
I want all the children in the world
to have a happy home like mine.
It makes me sad to know
that many do not have enough to eat
and don't have kind doctors and nurses
to make them well when they are ill.
Thank you for sending Jesus
to tell us about your loving care
for your big family.
Dear God,
I love you very much.

George Appleton

187 *God like a parent*

Dear God, who I feel is like my Father and my Mother,
I love my home and am lucky to be in one.
So my prayer today
is for all those children who haven't one.
Dear God, it seems to me that you yourself are a "home",
so will you please come as near as you can
to such homeless children?
And so, dear God, they can, though homeless,
be comforted by sights and sounds and feelings of home,
and their hearts may come to rest.

Donald Swann

188 *Baby coming home*

Dear Lord,
today, my baby brother came home from hospital.
He is very small and cries a lot.
Please help him to grow up quickly
so that I can play with him.

The elderly

189 *Elderly people see the truth of Jesus*

Then, after the purification had been completed in accordance with the Law of Moses, they brought him up to Jerusalem to present him to the Lord (as prescribed in the law of the Lord: "Every first-born male shall be deemed to belong to the Lord"), and also to make the offering as stated in the law: "A pair of turtle doves or two young pigeons."

There was at that time in Jerusalem a man called Simeon. This man was upright and devout, one who watched and waited for the restoration of Israel, and the Holy Spirit was upon him. It had been disclosed to him by the Holy Spirit that he would not see death until he had seen the Lord's Messiah. Guided by the Spirit he came into the temple; and when the parents brought in the child Jesus to do for him what was customary under the Law, he took him in his arms, praised God, and said:

"This day, Master, thou givest thy servant his discharge in peace; now thy promise is fulfilled.

For I have seen with my own eyes the deliverance which thou hast made ready in full view of all the nations: a light that will be a revelation to the heathen, and glory to thy people Israel."

The child's father and mother were full of wonder at what was being said about him. Simeon blessed them and said to Mary his mother, "This child is destined to be a sign which men reject; and you too shall be pierced to the heart. Many in Israel will stand or fall because of him, and thus the secret thoughts of many will be laid bare."

There was also a prophetess, Anna the daughter of Phanuel, of the tribe of Asher. She was a very old woman, who had lived seven years with her husband after she was first married, and then alone as a widow to the age of eighty-four. She never left the temple but worshipped day and night, fasting and praying. Coming up at that very moment, she returned thanks to God; and she talked about the child to all who were looking for the liberation of Jerusalem.

Luke 2. 22-38 (NEB)

190 *Care for the elderly*

Be with all those, O Lord, who care for the old;
give them patience and strength, gentleness and love,
that the dignity of all may be maintained,
for Jesus Christ's sake.

191 *Getting old*

Lord, bless those who are old and frail
that they may be sure of your strength.
Give us, and those who care for them,
patience and understanding and loving hearts.

192 *Grandparents*

Let the warmth and kindness of your love, O Lord,
surround our grandparents,
that they may be safe and at peace,
today and for always.

193 *Cherishing grandparents*

Thank you, Father, for our grandparents.
Teach us to be thankful for their kindness
and as they grow older may we cherish them
like they cherish us.

194 *On the death of a grandparent*

Dear Lord, thank you for grandparents.
My gran was fun.
She used to laugh a lot and read me stories.
She was warm and friendly.
I'll miss her now she's dead.
But I know I'm lucky —
some children never even meet their grandparents.
It's funny to think
that one day I'll be old like my gran.
I hope I'll be as smiley and kind as her.
Thank you, Lord, for grandparents.

195 *Our own attitudes to the elderly*

O God, help us to see and appreciate
the gifts of the elderly:
their wisdom and their experience;
and bring all generations closer together
that we may understand
and love one another.

196 *Old people*

There are some old people whose lives are like autumn,
mellow, quiet and wise.
Help us, Lord, to admire them
and to listen to them patiently.

The disabled

197 *Jesus the healer*

On another Sabbath he had gone to synagogue and was teaching. There happened to be a man in the congregation whose right arm was withered; and the lawyers and the Pharisees were on the watch to see whether Jesus would cure him on the Sabbath, so that they could find a charge to bring against him. But he knew what was in their minds and said to the man with the withered arm, 'Get up and stand out here.' So he got up and stood there. Then Jesus said to them, 'I put the question to you: is it permitted to do good or to do evil on the Sabbath, to save life or to destroy it?' He looked round at them all and then said to the man, 'Stretch out your arm.' He did so, and his arm was restored. But they were beside themselves with anger, and began to discuss among themselves what they could do to Jesus.

Luke 6. 6-11 (NEB)

198 *Mentally handicapped people*

Help us, O God,
to enter gently into the world
of mentally handicapped people,
that in humility we may learn from them
and share with them
in the beauty and mystery of your world.

199 *Caring for others*

Father, sometimes I get so bothered and worried about
myself that I forget others.
Forgive me. Keep me from being self-centred and
help me always to care for those who need my love
today, tomorrow and for ever ...

200 *Self-offering*

O loving Father,
I offer myself to be used by you
for the comforting of the sad,
the strengthening of the weak,
and the befriending of the lonely;
through Jesus Christ our Lord.

201 *The spirit of service*

O God, our heavenly Father, whose Son, our Lord Jesus
Christ,
took the form of a servant and became the Man for others;
give to us the same spirit of service
and help us to follow in his steps,
that with love and humility
we may give ourselves to those who need our help;
for the glory of your name.

Frank Colquhoun

202 *Prayer from a disabled child*

Lord, you were disabled
when you hung on the cross;
yet that is how you showed us God's love.
May the power of that love shine through my weakness,
my disability,
to show God's glory to the world.

Susan Mabe

203 *For disabled children*

When I meet and work with children
who are not so well and strong as I am,
help me, God, to help them in the right way,
so that we can all work together
and take our share, for Jesus' sake.

204 *Big hearts*

Give us big hearts, dear God;
big enough to embrace all mankind;
big enough to acknowledge our own weakness;
big enough to be humble;
big enough to acknowledge our need of each other;
big enough for you.

205 *A "halo" prayer*

Picture in your mind the person for whom you are praying;
then imagine that person surrounded by the light of God,
like a halo. Keep silence and after a while say,

>"Together, Lord,
>together all of us are surrounded by your love.
>Thank you."

Friends

206 *Jesus chooses his closest friends*

At that time Jesus went off to a mountain to pray. He stayed there all night, praying to God. The next morning, Jesus called his followers to him. He chose twelve of them, whom he named "apostles". They were Simon (Jesus named him Peter) and Andrew, Peter's brother; James and John, Philip and Bartholomew; Matthew, Thomas, James son of Alphaeus, and Simon (called the Zealot), Judas the son of James and Judas Iscariot. This Judas was the one who gave Jesus to his enemies.

Luke 8. 12-16 (ICB)

207 *Circle of friends*

A circle can be so strong and forbidding.
It's fine for those inside,
but for those outside it's not so good.
May our circles of friends
always be open to the needs of others,
so that we may be generous and not mean,
thoughtful and not spiteful;
for Jesus' sake.

208 *Needing God*

O Lord, never suffer us
to think that we can stand by ourselves
and not need thee.

John Donne

209 *Thankfulness for friends*

Lord God, thank you for all my friends,
for the jokes we share,
the games we play
and the work we do together.

210 *Loyalty*

Grant us, O Lord, loyalty of heart,
that as we demand that others should be faithful to us,
we also may be faithful to them;
for Jesus Christ's sake.

211 *Difficulties in friendship*

O God, I hate fighting with my friends,
but sometimes I get so mad
I could punch them on the nose —
like when they wreck my game or call me names,
or won't let me play with them.
Help me to remember that you love them
and help me love them too,
even when they're mean to me.

212 *Saying "No"*

Dear God, I find saying "Yes" so much easier
than saying "No"
and so when my friends ask me to do things that
I know are wrong
I curl up inside, frightened to say "No".
When I need to say "No",
when I ought to say "No",
give me the courage, O Lord — please.

213 *The well-being of friends*

O God, who by the grace of the Holy Ghost
has poured the gifts of love
into the hearts of thy faithful people;
grant unto them, whom thou hast given us
most dearly to love, health of body and soul,
that they may love thee with all their strength
and in happiness perform all thy good pleasure;
through Jesus Christ our Lord.

214 *Those without friends*

I can see them standing all alone,
at the bus-stop,
in the playground.
They have no friends —
and a bit of me is sorry,
and a bit of me is very glad that it's not me!
Help me, O God, to care for all who are lonely
and to share your love with everyone.

121

215 *Making new friends*

Lord Jesus, as I move to a new house and a new school,
please be with me and make me brave.
May I soon make new friends
and discover a whole new world of fun and friendship.

216 *Unkindness*

O Lord Jesus, we confess
that we are sometimes deliberately unkind to other people.
Forgive us and help us to show them your love.

217 *Blessing on friendship*

Loving Father, Creator of all things,
Author of all goodness, Source of all unifying love,
make us aware at this moment of your love for us.
Bless our world, our country, our friends, ourselves.
Enrich our leisure, enhance our work,
make noble our love for others
and grant that at all times and in all places,
in all things great and small, we may do thy perfect will;
through Jesus Christ our Lord.

218 *Friends far away*

O Lord, we bring to you our friends who live far away . . .
May they be aware of your blessing upon them,
and grant that,
although we are separated from them by great distances,
we may be aware of your love uniting us.
This we ask for Jesus' sake.

219 *Strong friendships*

Let our friendships be so strong, O Lord,
that they become a blessing to others . . .
Let our friendships be so open, O Lord,
that they may be a haven for others . . .
Let our friendships be so gentle, O Lord,
that they may bring peace to others . . .
for Jesus' sake.

220 *For the lonely*

Dear Lord Jesus, please bless those who are lonely.
Bless children who have no friends to play with,
and bless old people who have no-one to visit them.
Please let them understand
that you are always with them and always loving them.
Please help me
to be kind and friendly to lonely people.

221 *My friends*

My friends are those who listen when I am sad,
laugh with me when I am happy,
are quiet with me when I am tired
and who trust me.
God, protect them
and let me learn to trust them as they trust me.
Teach me to be as good a friend as they are to me.
And let me learn to treat you as the best of my friends,
and to trust you.

222 *Jesus and his friends*

Peter promised he would stay with you always, Lord,
and then he abandoned you
and felt ashamed.
I know that I might have done the same,
and so, as you forgave Peter,
giving him courage to proclaim your resurrection,
forgive me when I abandon my friends
and give me the courage to say I'm sorry,
to them
and to you.

People who help us

223 *Jesus the servant*

Jesus knew that the Father had given him complete power; he knew that he had come from God and was going to God. So he rose from the table, took off his outer garment, and tied a towel round his waist. Then he poured some water into a basin and began to wash his disciples' feet and dry them with the towel round his waist.

After Jesus had washed their feet, he put his outer garment back on and returned to his place at the table. "Do you understand what I have just done to you?" he asked. "You call me Teacher and Lord, and it is right that you do so, because that is what I am. I, your Lord and Teacher, have just washed your feet. You, then, should wash one another's feet. I have set an example for you, so that you will do just what I have done for you. I am telling you the truth: no slave is greater than his master, and no messenger is greater than the one who sent him. Now that you know this truth, how happy you will be if you put it into practice!

John 13. 3-5, 12-17 (GNB)

224 *Teachers*

Let your Holy Spirit rest upon all teachers, Lord,
that they may be guided by you
in thought and word and deed,
and reflect in their lives
your truth, your patience and your humble love.

225 *Fire-fighters*

There's a roar as the fire-engine
leaves the fire-station;
tyres squeal and sirens scream
as the fire-fighters prepare to tackle the blaze.

O God, give those brave men and women
the courage and skills they need
for their dangerous tasks,
and bless their families
that they too may be kept in your
patient love.

226 *Life-savers*

Almighty God, whose Son gave his life that we might live,
be with all who risk their lives for others
and grant them the knowledge of your supporting love,
for His sake.

227 *Farmers*

Lord of seed-time and harvest,
grant to those who farm
the skill to grow good food
and such wisdom in the use of the land
that it may be fruitful for the generations yet to come.

228 *Police*

O holy God and heavenly Father,
bless with your wisdom all those who uphold the law.
When they are perplexed, guide them;
when they are in danger, protect them;
when they are exhausted, uphold them;
that they may be people of integrity and truth,
working with us all for a better society.

229 *The armed forces*

Guide with your peace and your wisdom, O God,
those who defend our land.
May they never abuse their power
nor take to themselves the rights which belong to us.
At all times keep them loyal to your truth
and devoted to the cause of peace.

230 *Dustmen*

Dear God, may those who sweep and clean
and take away our rubbish
be assured of your love and our respect,
for you are the servant of all.

231 *For all who help*

Here comes a list, O God,
a list of those who help us,
a list of good and loving people.
Here we go. Are you ready?
Doctors, Nurses, Firemen, Policemen and women,
Teachers, Air -Sea Rescue Teams,
Life-boat crews,
Coast-guards . . .
Accept our prayers as though they were
"three cheers"
for we are very grateful for them all.

232 *Doctors and nurses*

Almighty God,
whose blessed Son Jesus Christ went about doing good,
and healing all manner of sickness
and all manner of disease among the people:
continue, we beseech thee, this his gracious work
among us in the hospitals of our land.
Cheer, heal and sanctify the sick;
to doctors and nurses grant skill, sympathy and patience;
and send down thy blessing
on all who labour to prevent suffering,
and to forward thy purposes of love;
through Jesus Christ our Lord.

1928 Prayer Book

Daily Life

School

233 Jesus the teacher

One day, as he was teaching the people in the temple and telling them the good news, the priests and lawyers, and the elders with them, came upon him and accosted him. 'Tell us', they said, 'by what authority you are acting like this; who gave you this authority?' He answered them, 'I have a question to ask you too: tell me, was the baptism of John from God or from men?' This set them arguing among themselves: 'If we say, "from God", he will say, "Why did you not believe him?" And if we say, "from men", the people will all stone us, for they are convinced that John was a prophet.' So they replied that they could not tell. And Jesus said to them, 'Neither will I tell you by what authority I act.'

Luke 20. 1-8 (NEB)

234 The school

Inside this school, O Lord, there are lots of people
trying to know and understand your world.
Give us courage when things are difficult,
hope when things seem gloomy
and joy when things go well.

235 *Blessing on a school*

Let thy blessing, O Lord,
rest upon our work in this school.
Teach us to seek after truth
and enable us to attain it;
but grant that
as we increase in knowledge of earthly things,
we may grow in knowledge of thee,
whom to know is life eternal;
through Jesus Christ our Lord.
Adapted from Thomas Arnold (1795-1842) of Rugby School

236 *The Spirit rests on the school*

Lord, let your Holy Spirit rest upon our school
that it may be a place of love and truth
where the weak are made strong,
and the strong learn humility,
and all of us learn the wisdom
that alone comes from you.

237 *God bless our school*

God bless our school;
bless those who teach,
bless those who learn,
and bless us all with the knowledge of your love;
through Jesus Christ our Lord.

238 *Opening eyes to truth*

Holy and loving God;
open our eyes to see you,
open our minds to trust you,
open our hearts to love you
this day and for evermore.

239 *Mirrors*

Father of love, make us like gleaming mirrors
so that we may reflect your marvellous light.

240 *Books*

We thank you, Father, for the authors and books
which have given us the greatest pleasure.
We remember their names before you now . . .
Help us to use words wisely and well,
expressing our thoughts in a clear and truthful way.

241 *Curiosity*

Father, I thank you
for the complex pleasures you have given us;
I thank you for filling us with curiosity;
keep me interested in everything
and then teach me thankfulness.

242   *Grace to work*

The things, good Lord, that we pray for
give us grace to work for;
through Jesus Christ our Lord.

243   *For those who have no school*

O Lord and heavenly Father,
we bring to you in our prayers
those children who have no schools
and no opportunity to learn;
may we be generous in caring for them
and share with them our learning and our wealth,
for all good things are given to us to share.

244   *Fair play*

O God, look upon our school with love,
that it may be a place of hope for the fearful,
a refuge for the despised
and a protection from the strong;
but above all make it a place where truth may flourish
and fair dealing abound
and life be lived to the full.

Child abuse and bullying

245 *Who is the greatest?*

At that time the disciples came to Jesus and asked, "Who is the greatest in the kingdom of Heaven?" He called a child, set him in front of them, and said, "I tell you this: unless you turn round and become like children, you will never enter the kingdom of Heaven. Let a man humble himself till he is like this child, and he will be the greatest in the kingdom of Heaven. Whoever receives one such child in my name receives me. But if a man is a cause of stumbling to one of these little ones who have faith in me, it would be better for him to have a millstone hung round his neck and be drowned in the depths of the sea. Alas for the world that such causes of stumbling arise!

Matthew 18. 1-7a (NEB)

246 *Suffering abuse*

Almighty God and heavenly Father,
protect with your mercy
those children who suffer at the hands of their parents;
give them wisdom and courage
that they may know whom they can trust
so that goodness and justice may prevail.

247 *Friends who are hurt*

Dearest God,
the knowledge that some of our friends may be being hurt
is more than we can bear.
Show us what we can do
to bring them your love,
your healing
and your concern for their good.

248 *Victims*

Holy God, those of us who are powerless look to you.
Give us strength and understanding
and the courage we need to live without fear.

249 *Fear*

O God, I hate being afraid;
there's the fluttering in the stomach,
the lurch as I see them come towards me,
and worst of all,
I hate myself for being their victim.
Show me the way through, O God,
that there may be justice for me and for them.

250 *Bullies*

Father in heaven, please let your love work
within the hearts of those who bully,
that they may cease from their cruelty
and learn to be at peace with themselves
and with others.

251 *Those who are frightened*

O God,
you are filled with tender love
for those who live in fear
— bless all children who live in fear:
afraid of someone at home;
afraid of someone at school;
afraid of a relation;
afraid of someone who has treated them wrongly.
Give all those children the wisdom
they need to know whom they can trust,
so that their fears can be heard,
and justice and truth prevail.
And then bring to their wounded minds and souls
the healing of your peace.

Journeys

252 *God is with us*

"Joshua, be strong and brave! You must lead these people so they can take their land. This is the land I promised their fathers I would give them. Be strong and brave. Be sure to obey all the teachings my servant Moses gave you. If you follow them exactly, you will be successful in everything you do. Always remember what is written in the Book of the Teachings. Study it day and night. Then you will be sure to obey everything that is written there. If you do this, you will be wise and successful in everything. Remember that I commanded you to be strong and brave. So don't be afraid. The Lord your God will be with you everywhere you go."

Joshua 1. 6-9 (ICB)

253 *Pilgrims*

Draw us nearer to you each day, O Lord,
for you are our purpose, our destiny.

254 *The way to God*

O Christ, who art the way to God,
teach us how to follow you.

255 *Bridges*

Suspend my life, O Lord, upon the pillars of your love,
making me graceful, useful and strong.

256 *Bridge-builders*

O God, Creator of man,
we thank you for the skills you have given us.
Teach us to use those skills with care,
so that the things we create may reflect your glory.

257 *Cyclists*

Father of all, be with us as we ride our bikes
and keep us calm and sensible
so that we neither endanger our own lives,
nor the lives of others.

258 *For the splendour of engines*

It's the purr and roar of the engines
that I love, O Lord;
all that power and speed
and the promise of arriving at new destinations.
For all who make engines
and all who maintain them,
accept our thanks and praise, O Lord.

259 *For those going away from home*

O Jesus, I want to ask you to watch over those I love
who are going away from me.
Take care of them on their journey;
guard them from harm while they are away,
and bring them home again happily and safely.

260 *A blessing for travellers*

May the road rise to meet you.
May the wind be always at your back.
May the sun shine warm upon your face,
the rains fall soft upon your fields and,
until we meet again,
may God hold you in the palm of his hand.

Traditional Celtic blessing

261 *Those at sea*

O God our Father, we pray for all who are at sea.
In storms, give them courage;
protect them from disaster;
and bring them safely home.
In the name of your son who stilled the tempest,
Jesus Christ our Lord.

262 *Trust in God*

I know, O God,
that wherever I travel,
you will be with me.
There is nowhere I can go,
no situation I can face,
which is outside your love and strength;
and so I commit myself
into your care and keeping
on this journey,
knowing that at all times
I am in your hands.

Villages and towns

263 *Living stones*

Rid yourselves, then, of all this evil; no more lying or
hypocrisy or jealousy or insulting language. Be like new-
born babies, always thirsty for the pure spiritual milk, so
that by drinking it you may grow up and be saved. As the
scripture says, "You have found out for yourselves how kind
the Lord is."

Come to the Lord, the living stone rejected by man as
worthless but chosen by God as valuable. Come as living
stones, and let yourselves be used in building the spiritual
temple, where you will serve as holy priests to offer spiritual
and acceptable sacrifices to God through Jesus Christ. For
the scripture says,

"I chose a valuable stone, which I am placing as the
cornerstone in Zion;

and whoever believes in him will never be dis-
appointed."

1 Peter 1. 1-6 (GNB)

264 *Rooftops*

The roofs of the town cascade down the hill.
Tiles like frozen waves form rough and lively patterns.
Dear God,
thank you for the people who make tiles and roofs.
Thank you for the patterns they create.

265 *Old buildings*

Lord of time, give us the wisdom
to appreciate the lives of our ancestors,
to learn from their mistakes
and to build on their good foundations.

266 *The parish church*

Lord, thank you for all those people
who have worshipped in this place.
May we, who have inherited their treasures,
continue their work of worship;
through Jesus Christ Our Lord.

267 *Shops*

God of all people and places, bless those who work in shops,
that their lives of service
may be signs of your love at work in the world;
through Jesus Christ,
who himself was the servant of all.

268 *My neighbour*

I am glad you made my neighbour different from me;
a different coloured skin, a different shaped face;
a different response to you.
I need my neighbour to teach me about you;
he knows all the things I don't know.

Monica Furlong

269 *The city*

O God, who ascended into the heavens
that you might fill all things,
stretch forth hands of blessing over this city
in which we live and work
and grant that your name may be glorified amongst us
and that through trade and commerce
we may offer to you the devotion of our lives;
through Jesus Christ our Lord.

270 *Cities*

Lord Jesus when you looked out at Jerusalem,
you wanted to enfold it in your loving arms:
look with pity and mercy upon our city;
bring to all who are in distress
the knowledge of your peace,
and to all who live and work here
the joy of your eternal presence,
O ever-living Lord.

271 *Rush and bustle*

It's the noise, O God:
the noise of cars,
the noise of trains,
noise of buses, noise of planes.
In all this rush and bustle and din,
keep all who live here free from sin
and grant us in the noise to hear
the love of Jesus drawing near.

272 *This is our town*

This is our town, O Lord,
roads roaring with traffic,
skies busy with planes,
streets crowded with people,
shops selling their wares,
trains sounding their hooters,
bikes ringing their bells,
people laughing and talking,
children skipping and shouting,
mothers pushing their prams,
fathers cleaning their cars,
grannies walking so slowly . . .

This is our town, O Lord.
Guard it for us and keep us safe,
now and forever. Amen.

Industry and commerce

273 Sowing and reaping

Do not be fooled: you cannot cheat God. A person harvests only what he plants. If he plants to satisfy his sinful self, his sinful self will bring him eternal death. But if he plants to please the Spirit, he will receive eternal life from the Spirit. We must not become tired of doing good. We will receive our harvest of eternal life at the right time. We must not give up! When we have the opportunity to help anyone, we should do it.

Galatians 6. 7-10a (ICB)

274 God's world

Lord, you have taught us
that the world is yours, and those who dwell on it.
Hear us, therefore, as we pray for the life of the world;
that every nation may seek the way that leads to peace;
that human rights and freedom may everywhere be respected;
and that the earth's resources
may be ungrudgingly shared among all men.
We ask this through Jesus Christ our Lord.

275 *Scientists*

Direct, O Lord, with thine own loving wisdom
all men of thought and science,
that they may more and more
unveil the wondrous things of thy law
and draw all men to adore thee
with mind and heart and soul; through Jesus Christ.

276 *Factories*

Father, thank you for all the good things made in factories.
May we never be so carefree in the use of things
that we forget the toil that has gone into making them.

277 *The media*

Father, you spoke the word and the universe came to life.
Teach us to use words with respect and care,
knowing the great good and the great harm that words can do.

278 *Building the Kingdom*

Jesus, Lord and brother, at Nazareth you grew to manhood,
busy in the sunlit workshop with eye and hand and brain,
yet ever dreaming of a kingdom to be built,
wordwide, eternal, not made with hands:
help us to grow in wisdom, loving the things of heaven,
seeing the world, as with your eyes, at its true value;
for the sake of yourself, our Saviour Jesus Christ.

Edward Sedding

279 *At the market*

O God our Father, we pray thee to bless this market
and all who buy and sell in it.
Be with the traders also, as they travel from place to place.
Protect them and us in body and soul.
Help us to deal honestly and fairly with one another,
so that everyone may benefit from the trade that is done,
and live together in peace and prosperity,
giving thee thanks for all thy gifts.
For the sake of Jesus Christ our Lord.

280 *Changes*

O Father, all time is in your hands.
May we hold on to that which is good from the past,
be aware of the joys of the present,
and rejoice in the boundless possibilities of the future.

281 *Industry*

Heavenly Father, creator of the world,
guide with your wisdom
those who create the wealth of our land,
that they may have a care for the earth,
a concern for their employees
and deal justly with all.

282 *Unemployment*

The day is there and the sunshine,
with steamers in the harbour,
but is there work?
Others have friends,
others have money,
and I stand nearby unemployed.
Dear God, can't you give me work in the harbour
to have money for wife and children?
To put my little bit in your basket next Sunday?
Please give me work, good Lord Jesus.
We praise you. Amen.

Prayer of a young Ghanaian Christian

283 *Coal and stone*

Lord God, bless the miners of coal and stone;
keep them safe in their work;
give them courage in danger
and strength for their labours.
May we understand all that they do
and work with them for the benefit of our world.

284 *Oil*

Heavenly King, may those who bring us our oil
treat the riches of our world with care;
work for the well-being of our generation
and for the good of children yet to be born.

285 *Gas*

Lord of creation, give to those who tap the energies of our world
thankfulness for your bounty and a concern for the environment;
for all that has been, and all that is, are yours . . .

Leisure

286 *Singing and dancing*

'How can I describe the people of this generation? What are they like? They are like children sitting in the market-place and shouting at each other,

"We piped for you and you would not dance."

"We wept and wailed, and you would not mourn."

For John the Baptist came neither eating bread nor drinking wine, and you say, "He is possessed." The Son of Man came eating and drinking, and you say, "Look at him! a glutton and a drinker, a friend of tax-gatherers and sinners!" And yet God's wisdom is proved right by all who are her children."

Luke 7.31-35 (NEB)

287 *Harmony with nature*

God of the green pastures and still waters,
help my heart to beat in time
with the quiet music of your creation.

288 *Sea and sand*

Dear Father God,
there's the smell of the sea-side in the air;
there's sand beneath our feet;
cliffs and rocks on the edge of the bay;
the cry of seagulls in a pure blue sky;
and all I want to do is rush
to the water's edge
and splash my happiness all around.
Accept my joy as my prayer,
O God, my Creator and my King.

289 *Fireworks*

Here are our fireworks, O God,
— a Catherine wheel that spins around,
a rocket that flashes up into the dark night air,
a Roman fountain spraying colours everywhere.
And you, Creator God,
have given us a universe,
of galaxies like Catherine wheels
and comets like rockets
and stars and suns and planets like Roman fountains.
We rejoice in the glory of fireworks,
those on earth
and those in the heavens,
and give you thanks and praise.

290 *Sport*

Thank you, Lord, that we can run and jump.
Thank you that we can dive and swim.
Thank you for designing our bodies so that we can play
all kinds of games.
Thank you for good feelings we have
when we have exercised well.
Help us to keep our bodies fit and healthy.
In Jesus' name, Amen.

291 *Television*

There it sits in the corner of the room,
flickering images of life and laughter,
of sadness and disaster . . .
O God, bless the makers of TV programmes;
give them wise judgement,
and a full appreciation
of the hidden glories and mystery of our world.
Keep them ever mindful of their power
to hurt but also to heal,
to destroy but also to make new
and above all,
give them a love of truth,
a love of humanity
and a love for you, O God.

292 *Singing and swinging*

Lord, I can skip and jump and shout and S I N G !
I can skip and clap and stamp and S W I N G !
Thank you for making me alive!

293 *In the park*

A dog barks;
some boys are chasing a football;
some girls are running to the swimming pool;
old people sit on benches in the sun
and it's a good place to be.
Bless you, O God, for the makers of parks.

294 *Football*

I lie in the bath,
soaking the mud off my knees
and remembering the goal I almost scored,
and the time I passed the ball brilliantly
(tho' no-one saw),
and the way I made space for myself —
and I'm just glad, O God, glad to be alive.
Thank you.

295 *Rugby*

They ran on to the pitch,
like gods (if you'll forgive the expression)
smelling of sweat and confidence and liniment,
and when the game began,
it was like watching music,
and we shouted until we were hoarse
and then went home satisfied and had a huge warm tea . . .
Just thought I'd tell you, God,
for you surely take pleasure in pleasure.

296 *Tennis*

I've tried grunting when I serve
to see if it helps;
I even wear wrist-bands and a head-band
but I still can't volley like I want to . . .
O God, bless you for all the things I can do
but please give me the patience to improve . . .
soon.

297 *Cricket*

Green grass,
white clothes,
and under the shade of the tree,
out of the dazzling sun
sits an old man wearing a panama hat,
watching
and remembering
and giving wistful thanks
for the boundless grace of youth.
O God, for the pleasures of our world,
we give you thanks and praise.

298 *Skipping in the playground*

Listen to the sound of the skipping rope . . .
Listen to the sound of feet,
tapping on the floor as they skip . . .
Listen to the words of the rhyme . . .
Clap to the rhythm . . .

When the rope whirs round and the words keep time,
clap, clap, clap, clap, clap, clap, clap.
Then's the moment for an ancient rhyme,
clap, clap, clap, clap, clap, clap, clap.
God's in his heaven, and Jesus is King.
This is a rhyme that we can sing,
so clap your hands and stamp your feet,
our prayers keep dancing to a skipping beat.

299 *Games indoors*

This is a game we play at home . . .
It is called . . .

When we play: Thank you, God.
When we laugh: Thank you, God.
When we think: Thank you, God.
When we learn: Thank you, God.

300 *Balloons*

Praying is like tapping a balloon up to God. Write on a balloon in felt-tip all the words you want to share with God: favourite words, favourite games . . . Tap the balloon up into the air and . . .

"Thank you God for the joy and pleasure of games".

Shopping

301 *Piling up riches*

A man in the crowd said to Jesus, "Teacher, tell my brother to divide with me the property our father left us."

Jesus answered him, "My friend, who gave me the right to judge or to divide the property between you two?"

And he went on to say to them all, "Watch out and guard yourselves from every kind of greed; because a person's true life is not made up of the things he owns, no matter how rich he may be."

Then Jesus told them this parable: "There was once a rich man who had land which bore good crops. He began to think to himself, 'I haven't anywhere to keep all my crops. What can I do? This is what I will do,' he told himself; 'I will tear down my barns and build bigger ones, where I will store all my corn and other goods. Then I will say to myself, Lucky man! You have all the good things you need for many years. Take life easy, eat, drink and enjoy yourself!' But God said to him, 'You fool! This very night you will have to give up your life; then who will get all these things you have kept for yourself?'"

And Jesus concluded, "This is how it is with those who pile up riches for themselves but are not rich in God's sight."

Luke 12. 13-21 (GNB)

302 *Shopping for food*

We go shopping at . . .
My favourite foods are . . .

Lord in heaven, thank you for our food shops —
and for the colours, the lights, the bustle;
help us, as we buy our food,
to remember the hungry, the poor and the refugees,
and to do something to help them.

303 *Shopping for clothes*

My favourite clothes are . . .

In yellow boots and red cagoules,
In purple socks and training shoes,
In sweaters green and jumpers blue,
may God bless me and God bless you.

304 *Shopping for shoes*

My favourite shoes are . . .
This is what I can do in my shoes. I can hop, skip . . .

Father bless the makers of shoes,
and help us, wherever we go,
to walk in your way, in safety and in love.

305 *Shopping for toys*

My favourite toy-shop is . . .
I like this toy best because . . .

God bless those who help to make life enjoyable and fun
and give us all thankful and generous hearts.

306 *Shopping for videos/records/tapes/books*

My favourite video/record shop is . . .
My favourite video/record is . . .

The people film the video —
the editors cut it into special lengths —
the scientists process it . . .
People put it into boxes —
the boxes are driven to the shop —
the shop sells it . . .

We depend on each other, Lord;
help us to treat everyone with respect and encouragement,
so that our fellowship one with another
is like your love for us — strong and good.

307 *Ice-Cream*

For water-ices, cheap but good,
that find us in a thirsty mood;
for ices made of milk or cream
that slip down smoothly as a dream;
for cornets, sandwiches and pies
that make the gastric juices rise;
for ices bought in little shops
or at the kerb from him who stops;
for chanting of the sweet refrain:
"chocolate, strawberry or plain?"
We thank thee, Lord, who sends with the heat
this cool deliciousness to eat.

308 *Shopkeepers*

Let your blessing rest softly upon those who serve us in shops,
and may we treat them with gratitude and courtesy
for their service to us and to others,
for Jesus' sake, the Servant of all.

The Seasons

Spring

309 *A lover's song*

The winter is over; the rains have stopped;
in the countryside the flowers are in bloom.
This is the time for singing;
the song of doves is heard in the fields.
Figs are beginning to ripen;
the air is fragrant with blossoming vines.

Song of Solomon 2. 11-13a (GNB)

310 *The buds on a tree*

The buds on the branch are like tiny green missiles
waiting to burst open . . .
Dear God, for the power of new life
surging through our world,
we bless and praise your holy name.

311 *Sunshine on a new-mown lawn*

Lord, you bathe the world with light;
bathe our hearts and our lives
with your peace, your love, your beauty.

312 *Bird-song*

This morning we heard the song of . . .
O Lord, when we're so happy,
we want to sing and skip and turn cartwheels;
help us to hug your world with love.

313 *Spring cleaning*

The sun's shining, the dusters are out
and we're making everything squeaky clean . . .
Lord of all, as we clean and shine and polish —
make our lives brilliant for you.

314 *Yellow*

Yellow daffodils . . .
Like fragile stars, like a captured sunbeam,
the daffodils dance in the breeze . . .
Lord, for the gold of bright new life,
we praise your name, O God.

315 *Red*

Red tulips . . .
The bright red cups of tulips receive the sun and the rain . . .
so may our lives be open to your love, O Lord our God.

316 *Ducks quacking*

Ducks walk like this . . .
These are the sounds they make . . .
When our prayers can only waddle,
when we can't think or say beautiful things —
accept even our waddling words
for they are ours, O God,
and the best we can sometimes do.

317 *Laughter in the street*

The sun's shining; it's a blue-sky day
and in the street
people are talking and smiling and laughing.
For loud voices, soft voices,
for kind voices, gentle voices,
for peals of laughter and silent smiles;
we thank you, heavenly Father.

318 *Planting new seeds*

In our garden we have planted . . .
The seeds are very, very tiny.
Dear God,
you have locked up so much life in such tiny spaces,
we are astonished when we think about it.
Let our astonishment be our prayer of thanks.

319 *Fresh and clean*

Thank you, Father, that Spring is a picture of your beauty.
Thank you for flowers and sunshine,
and the new life that Spring brings.
I pray that you would cleanse us,
so that we are fresh and new in you each day.
Amen.

320 *Pippa's song*

The year's at the Spring,
and the day's at the morn;
morning's at seven;
the hill-side dew-pearl'd;
the lark's on the wing;
the snail's on the thorn;
God's in his heaven —
all's right with the world!
Robert Browning

Summer

321 *Trusting in God*

Jesus said to his followers, "So I tell you, don't worry about the food you need to live. Don't worry about the clothes you need for your body. Life is more important than food. And the body is more important than clothes. Look at the birds. They don't plant or harvest. They don't save food in houses or barns. But God takes care of them. And you are worth much more than birds. None of you can add any time to your life by worrying about it. If you cannot do even the little things, then why worry about the big things? Look at the wild flowers. See how they grow. They don't work or make clothes for themselves. But I tell you that even Solomon, the great and rich king, was not dressed as beautifully as one of these flowers. God clothes the grass in the field like that. That grass is living today, but tomorrow it will be thrown into the fire. So you know how much more God will clothe you. Don't have so little faith! Don't always think about what you will eat and what you will drink. Don't worry about it. All the people in the world are trying to get those things. Your Father knows that you need them. The thing you should seek is God's kingdom. Then all the other things you need will be given to you.

Luke 12. 22-31 (ICB)

322 *The hum of insects*

When we are very, very still and quiet
we can hear the buzzing and humming of insects . . .
Dear Lord, it's a strange and miraculous world:
so much life, so much sound,
so much we don't understand.

323 *The chatter of sparrows*

The young sparrows are being fed,
their wings are beating,
they open their mouths very wide . . .
Lord of the sparrows,
help us to realise how much you love each one of us
just because we are.

324 *Grasshoppers*

The grasshoppers click and whirr like tiny green machines
lost in a miniature jungle . . .
As grasshoppers signal across their world,
so we signal our praise to you, O God
of the infinite universe, O God
at the centre of life.

325 *Enjoying the weather*

Lord, let your love and your joy shine upon us
and make our hearts glad — this lovely day and for ever.

326 *Seaside*

These are the seaside things we like to do . . .

for buckets and spades, for sunshine and shade,
for sand in the toes, for cream on the nose,
for jumping the tide, for having a ride,
for laughter and fun, praise God every one.

327 *Games*

Our favourite games are . . .

For cricket and tennis:	we thank you, O Lord.
For swimming and running:	we thank you, O Lord.
For lying and thinking:	we thank you, O Lord.
For talking and dreaming:	we thank you, O Lord.
For all that makes summer so lovely:	we thank you, O Lord.

328 *Whites and pinks*

When we have good weather we wear these colours . . .

For the lightness of our summer clothes,
for being able to move so much more easily,
for the joy of summer freedom,
we thank you, dearest God.

329 *Turquoise and purple*

When the sun is setting
and the sky changes colour very, very slowly
and with great beauty,
accept our quiet joy as our thanksgiving to you,
O Lord our God.

330 *Summer days*

The sun is golden in a pure blue sky,
the grass in the meadows ripples softly in the breeze,
a sky-lark pierces the air with his sweet song,
and in the hedgerows butterflies bask in the warmth.
And everything,
everything,
seems to be singing its own song of praise
to you, our Lord and our God.

331 *What a wonderful world!*

To see a World in a Grain of Sand
and a Heaven in a Wild Flower,
hold Infinity in the palm of your hand
and Eternity in an hour.

William Blake

Autumn

332 Gathering in the harvest

Be sure you know how your sheep are doing.
Pay close attention to the condition of your cattle.
Riches will not continue for ever.
Nor do governments continue for ever.
Bring in the hay. Let the new grass appear.
Gather the grass from the hills.
Make clothes from the lambs' wool.
Sell some goats to buy a field.
There will be plenty of goat's milk
to feed you and your family.

Proverbs 27. 23-27a (ICB)

333 Scuffing through leaves

The leaves go scrinch, scrunch,
minch, munch,
as we walk through the woods and the parks.
Thank you, God, for the laughing pleasure
of walking through falling leaves.

334 *Raining leaves*

Leaves sigh,
whisper,
glide
and flop to the ground.
Thank you, Lord, for the surprising
and quiet sounds of the world.

335 *Dying flowers*

Out in the garden
the flowers are turning from blue and purple to gold, to rust . . .
It's a bit sad, Lord, when lovely things die,
so help us to remember the promise of spring.

336 *Fruits of autumn*

It's time for playing conkers.
On the outside the shell is like . . .
The conker itself is like . . .
Thank you God for the beauty beneath the surface of things.

337 *In praise of Autumn*

We praise you, God, for golden leaves.
We praise you, God, for gentle mists.
We praise you, God, for apples and fruit.
We praise you, God, for chestnuts and conkers.
We praise you, God, for a glorious world.

338 *Autumn is a lovely season*

There are golden leaves carpeting the pavements,
conkers glistening dark and rich,
spiders' webs laced with dew,
and the air is moist and sharp on the skin;
on such days of mellow beauty
I just want to give you thanks, O God,
for your wonderful world.

339 *The days are getting shorter*

The world is beginning to settle down
to a thankful sleep, O God . . .
the earth has given us her harvest,
the barns are filled with grain
and now it's time for quietness and rest,
building up strength for the winter
and spring to come.
For the wise and gentle rhythms of life
we thank you, our Father and our God.

340 *A windy day*

We cannot see the wind blowing;
we can only see the trees bending in its path;
we can only see the ripples stirring the surface
of the water.

We cannot see your Spirit, Lord,
but only the movement in people's lives
caused by your love.

341 *A misty morning*

This morning the mist was softly gliding
around the lamp-posts and trees.
Everything looked different . . .
Thank you, God, for the unexpected jewels of your world.

342 *Grey skies*

No sun. No blue patches. No cotton wool clouds,
just heavy skies hanging low . . .
Father, Lord of all creation, when we can't seem to find you,
help us to realise that even on the dullest day
your presence is truly with us, deep, deep inside.

343 *Blackberries*

The hedges are thick with brambles . . .
For all the fruits of the wood and the hedge
we praise you, heavenly Father.

344 *Fog*

On this foggy day, dear Lord,
bless all those who have to travel,
that they may be kept safe
and free from all dangers.

345 *Apples*

The apples are being brought in to store.
They look like . . . They smell like . . .
They feel like . . .
God and Lord of the apple trees,
you have given us the fruits of the earth:
help us to share the bounty of harvest
with everyone everywhere.

Winter

346 *Praising God in the snow*

Praise the Lord from the earth,
you water-spouts and ocean depths;
fire and hail and snow and ice,
gales of wind obeying his voice;

Psalm 148. 7-8 (NEB)

347 *Snow*

The snow has blanketed the world
with a rare and lovely softness.
We praise you, God,
for the pure white beauty of snow.

348 *Snow-balling*

The snow whizzes through the air:
our hands get so cold we could cry
and the world is a mixture of crazy happiness
and freezing pain.
Dear God, bless those who find snow a real hazard
and keep them as safe as you can.

349   *Snow-clothes*

When it snows we have to wear special clothes . . .
We wear . . .
It makes us feel . . .
We walk like . . .
God, bless the makers of clothes
that keep us warm and dry and snug.
It feels very good.

350   *Ice on the roads*

This day the roads and pavements are very dangerous . . .
In the casualty wards of the hospitals
doctors and nurses will be very busy:
grant them, dear Lord, wisdom, skill and understanding
in all that they do.

351 *Breath freezing on the air*

When we are outside our breath freezes on the air;
we blow "smoke";
we are dragons breathing fire . . .

God, your Holy Spirit is the breath of life:
may He live within us,
bringing us your peace, your joy and your energy.

352   *A grey and heavy day*

Today, dear God, the clouds are grey,
the roads are grey, the fields are grey —
all the colour seems to have drained away.
On grey days, keep us content and happy,
so that our world becomes a bit brighter.

353   *Crisp, clear mornings*

The sky is an icy blue,
the hedges are edged with silver,
the sun bounces light around everything . . .
Thank you, God,
for the unexpected brilliance of a lovely day.

354   *Dark and misty afternoons*

When we go home tonight,
the sky will be getting dark,
everything will be sombre and dull . . .
On the dark, dark evenings, Lord, give us light hearts,
that even in the darkness we may rejoice in beauty.

355   *Starlight*

Lord God,
the heavens are full of your glory and your power —
bless you for life.

356 *Moonlight*

Soft, pale moonlight bathes the world —
and all is very, very quiet.
God, let your peace be in our minds
as softly as the moonlight . . .

357 *Hot toast*

Brown toast, white toast,
butter spread on cool toast,
black toast, scraped toast,
but best of all is *hot* toast . . .
so, Lord . . .
three cheers for toast.

358 *Coats in cloakrooms*

We have hung up our coats on the pegs —
the cloakroom has a special winter smell . . .
the smell is like . . .
Thank you, God, for the warmth and comfort of our school;
bless those who look after it
that it may always be a place of welcome
and safety for children.

359 *Winter games*

During the winter we play these games . . .
For football and running: we praise you, O God.
For jumping and skipping: we praise you, O God.
For skating and sliding: we praise you, O God.
For all that makes winter so special: we praise you, O God.

360 *Winter thaw*

I feel bitterly cold, O God,
cold outside,
cold inside.
I'm miserable, locked up, glum . . .
and what I need to feel
is the warmth of your sunshine
— sunshine for my body
and sunshine for my soul
so that I can live with joy in my heart
and the laughter of the universe
in my soul.

Weather

361 *The still, small voice*

"Go out and stand before me on top of the mountain," the Lord said to him. Then the Lord passed by and sent a furious wind that split the hills and shattered the rocks — but the Lord was not in the wind. The wind stopped blowing and then there was an earthquake — but the Lord was not in the earthquake. After the earthquake, there was a fire — but the Lord was not in the fire. And after the fire there was the soft whisper of a voice.

1 Kings 19. 11-12 (GNB)

362 *On a rainy day*

Father, today we splashed through puddles,
felt the rain on our faces,
and watched the water gurgling in the gutters.
Thank you for the rain,
for its gentle kindness,
for the fun we have . . .
It's good, because you made it.

363 *Floods*

Lord, on the television news we saw the floods,
and people sitting on the roofs of their houses.
Please take care of them, and help us to help them,
especially the children and the very old.

364 *Rainbows*

Lord,
the rainbow arched across the dark, dark sky
and it reminded me of you —
a beautiful bridge between the earth and heaven.
Thank you, Lord,
for the glory of rainbows.

365 *A sunny day*

Father, when I got up today
the sun was shining,
and the birds were singing.
I put on my sun-shiney clothes
and felt very happy.
Thank you for the sparkle and glitter of sunshine.

366 *Bringer of life*

Lord,
the sun is full of energy
bringing us life,
making seeds grow;
Make us like the sun,
radiant with the glory of being alive,
for Jesus' sake.

367 *Looking at sunshine streaming through a window*

Lord, there's a patch of sun on the . . .
In it I can see things more clearly.
The dust dancing, the colours in the room.
Just as the sun shines in our room,
may your love shine in our hearts
and make us beautiful for you.

368 *Excitement*

Lord, the wind is bending the trees,
blowing litter around the streets.
People struggle to walk against it,
but I love it when it's windy
and I want to run and laugh.
Thank you for the excitement of a windy day.

369 *Closing my eyes*

If I close my eyes, Lord, and listen,
I can hear the wind in the trees;
I can hear it roaring and rustling.
I can hear it crashing and creeping.
I can hear it sighing and singing.
Thank you for the music in the wind around the world.

370 *A Hurricane*

Almighty God,
be with all those who have suffered so much in the hurricane —
those who are injured,
those who are homeless,
those who are frightened.
Give your strength and comfort to them,
that they may know your peace,
for Jesus' sake.

371 *A gentle breeze*

The leaves on the birch tree are dancing;
in the wheatfields the corn ripples
like a golden and gentle sea.
Thank you for the soft beauty of summer breezes.

372 *A gale at sea*

On this day of gales and storms,
be with all those, Lord, who work at sea,
that they may be skilful and brave
and come home safely in calmer days;
through Jesus Christ our Lord.

373 *The warmth of the sun*

Lord, the sun makes us feel so good!
Its light brightens up our lives.
Thank you for lovely sunny days and bright blue skies.
Thank you for the sun which warms us
and helps everything to grow.
You are like the sun, Lord.
You warm us with your love and help us to grow.
Let your light shine in our lives.
Amen.

The Christian Year

Advent

374 *A story of five wise and five foolish virgins*

"At that time the Kingdom of heaven will be like this. Once there were ten girls who took their oil lamps and went to meet the bridegroom. Five of them were foolish and the other five were wise. The foolish ones took their lamps but did not take any extra oil with them, while the wise ones took containers full of oil for their lamps. The bridegroom was late in coming, so the girls began to nod and fall asleep.

"It was already midnight when the cry rang out, 'Here is the bridegroom! Come and meet him!' The ten girls woke up and trimmed their lamps. Then the foolish ones said to the wise ones 'Let us have some of your oil, because our lamps are going out.' 'No, indeed,' the wise ones answered, 'there is not enough for you and us. Go to the shop and buy some for yourselves.' So the foolish girls went off to buy some oil; and while they were gone, the bridegroom arrived. The five girls who were ready went in with him to the wedding feast, and the door was closed.

"Later the other girls arrived. 'Sir, sir! Let us in!' they cried out. 'Certainly not! I don't know you', the bridegroom answered."

And Jesus concluded, "Be on your guard, then, because you do not know the day or the hour."

Matthew 25. 1-13 (GNB)

The Advent Candles

Prayers to be used when each one is lit:

375 *The first candle*

Lord, as we prepare for Christmas, may this candle remind us of your light.

376 *The second candle*

Lord, as we prepare for Christmas, may this candle remind us of your peace.

377 *The third candle*

Lord, as we prepare for Christmas, may this candle remind us of your joy.

378 *The fourth candle*

Lord, as we prepare for Christmas, may this candle remind us of your love — for us and for all people everywhere.

379 *The circular candle-holder*

May this crown of fire encircle the world with your light, your peace, your joy and your love — for you are our God for ever and ever.

380 *Advent expectancy*

In the darkness we can see the tiniest glimmer of light.
We're in a tunnel, a long, dark tunnel,
but at the end there is the light of Christmas.

As we journey towards that light,
keep us unafraid of the darkness.
Give us courage and honesty
in facing the truths of our world,
so that we may come to the Christ child
with our lives full of hope.

381 *Waiting for God*

Lord God,
you promised that you would come to us:
be with us in the silence of our hearts,
in the depths of our imagination,
at the centre of our lives
and fill us with your love, now and for evermore.

382 *Listening to God*

In the Bible, Lord,
your stories sparkle with life;
may your words make us brilliant in word and deed,
that we may bring light to the world.

383 *Being judged by God*

Heavenly Father,
your light overcomes darkness;
take everything in my life that is dark
and transform it into glory;
through Jesus Christ our Lord.

384 *The light of Christ*

Lord our God,
on the first day of creation
you made the light that scatters all darkness.
Let Christ, the Light of Lights,
hidden from all eternity,
shine at last on your people
and free us from the darkness of sin.
Fill our lives with good works,
as we go out to meet your son,
so that we may rejoice to welcome him at his coming.
We ask this in the name of Jesus the Lord.

385 *An evening prayer*

O God, full of love, hear my prayer.
If we have done things which shame us,
show us the right way.
Thank you that the love which surrounded us
all day goes with us into the peace of night.

Christmas

386 *The birth of Jesus*

At that time the Emperor Augustus ordered a census to be
taken throughout the Roman Empire. When this first census
took place, Quirinius was the governor of Syria. Everyone,
then, went to register himself, each to his own town.

Joseph went from the town of Nazareth in Galilee to
the town of Bethlehem in Judaea, the birthplace of King
David. Joseph went there because he was a descendant of
David. He went to register with Mary, who was promised in
marriage to him. She was pregnant, and while they were in
Bethlehem, the time came for her to have her baby. She gave
birth to her first son, wrapped him in strips of cloth and laid
him in a manger — there was no room for them to stay in
the inn.

Luke 2. 1-7 (GNB)

387 *Party games*

Our favourite party-games are . . .
When we are so happy
that we don't know what to do with ourselves,
keep your still peace at the centre of our hearts, Lord — please.

388 *For those who can't go to parties*

God our Father, Heavenly King,
let us never be so self-centred
that we forget those who cannot go to parties,
and teach us how we may more justly share
the joys of the world.

389 *Decorating the tree*

These are the things we love:
the tinsel glinting . . .
the lights in the branches . . .
the baubles turning very, very slowly . . .
Lord, thank you for the deep, deep promise of Christmas.

390 *Collecting the tree*

Dearest God, may this tree,
strong and green and lovely,
be a sign to us of your everlasting love
and your joy in our world.

The Christmas Nativity Play

391 *The inn-keeper*

Lord, when I shut the door in the play,
may I remember to keep my life open to you —
for you are the surprise and joy of the world.

392 *The shepherds*

Lord, when we are faced by the angels,
help us to be aware of your true and holy glory —
for you are the splendour of the world.

393 *The angels*

Lord, when we bring the good news to Mary,
help us to be brilliant for you —
for you are the light of the world.

394 *The kings*

Lord, when we bring our gifts to the baby Jesus,
help us to give our lives to you —
for you are the true King of the world.

395 *Mary and Joseph*

Lord, when we welcome the child Jesus into our home,
help us to welcome him into our hearts —
for you are the love of our world.

The Shepherds

396 *The shepherd David*

O Holy God,
you called your servant David from being a shepherd
to be the king of your chosen people;
teach us how to be shepherds of kindness
and kings of truth in our lives.

397 *The Good Shepherd*

Lord Jesus, the Good Shepherd,
you look for those who have strayed and are lost;
look after our lives so that we become your friends
and stay close to you today and for ever.

398 *The Bethlehem shepherds*

If only we could have been there, Lord,
on that hillside . . .
We should have heard the sheep baa-ing;
the dogs barking . . .
the silence of the night —
and then, stars —
full of your glory
and the sounds of peace and goodwill . . .
"Glory to God in the highest . . ."

399 *The shepherds at the manger*

Father, as those first shepherds knelt at the cradle,
may we kneel quietly before you
just because we love you —
our God and our King.

400 *Shepherds today*

On all the hills of the world there are shepherds
caring for the sheep.
Take care of them, Lord,
and keep them aware that,
just as they look after their sheep,
so you look after them and us,
O Good Shepherd of our souls . . .

The Animals

401 *The donkey*

Lord God, maker of me,
keep me sure-footed and steady
that Mary may come safe to the inn.

402 *The camel*

Lord God, maker of me,
guide me carefully and slowly
that my king may find the Christ-child and rejoice.

403 *The elephant*

Lord God, maker of me,
keep me clear of all mice,
that my king may kneel quietly
before the child Jesus in worship.

404 *The sheep*

Lord God, maker of me,
let no dogs bark at me,
no crows caw at me,
no wolves howl at me —
for I want to be there with the rest
and see your son, my best shepherd.

Messengers

405 *Angel Gabriel*

Dear God,
may we hear all that you want to say to us,
and live gloriously for you and for our fellow men.

406 *The choir of angels*

Almighty Creator,
open our eyes to the glories of the world.
May we always be ready to be surprised by the universe
and to see your hand at work in everything . . .

407 *Friends calling*

We had some friends call . . .
they had come from . . .
They told us about . . .
Dearest God, thank you for the good messages
that travel with our friends.
Help us to learn from each other
and to enjoy the good things of your world
with thankfulness.

408 *Sad messages*

Sometimes people have to pass on sad messages —
like police, doctors, nurses, friends, vicars . . .
God be with all messengers
who this day are the bearers of sad news —
may they be wise and true
and very compassionate with those who suffer.

409 *Lord, now lettest thous they servant . . .*

When the old man, Simeon, had seen you, dear Lord,
he was very happy.
Thank you for him.
Thank you for his poem.
Thank you for the promise of his message.

410 *Sharing the songs of angels*

O God, our loving Father,
help us rightly to remember the birth of Jesus,
that we may share in the songs of the angels,
the gladness of the shepherds,
and the worship of the wise men.
May the Christmas morning
make us happy to be your children,
and the Christmas evenings
bring us to our beds with grateful thoughts,
forgiving and forgiven, for Jesus' sake.

Robert Louis Stevenson

411 *Sharing human suffering*

Lord Jesus Christ,
you shared human suffering
to reveal your Father's love:
draw near to those for whom Christmas brings little joy —
the hungry, the suffering, the lonely, and the bereaved;
may they find joy and hope in you.

412 *The biggest surprise*

Sometimes the most exciting things happen
not with noise and bustle
but in the still, small joys of the unexpected.
And in the glory of starlight,
out on the hills,
shepherds sensed that a miracle
was about to happen
and suddenly the cold night air
was filled with music
and the laughter of angels swept the earth
for the Christ-child was born,
Emmanuel,
God with us
— and in that birth
came our new life.
Alleluia, Lord,
Alleluia.

413 *Peace to all*

O God, you desire to enfold
both heaven and earth in a single peace.
Let the design of your great love
lighten upon the waste of our angers and sorrows;
and give peace to your church,
peace among nations,
peace in our homes,
and peace in our hearts;
through Jesus Christ our Lord.

Epiphany

414 *The coming of the Magi*

Jesus was born in the town of Bethlehem in Judaea, during the time when Herod was king. Soon afterwards, some men who studied the stars came from the east to Jerusalem and asked, "Where is the baby born to be the king of the Jews? We saw his star when it came up in the east, and we have come to worship him."

When King Herod heard about this, he was very upset, and so was everyone else in Jerusalem. He called together all the chief priests and teachers of the Law and asked them, "Where will the Messiah be born?"

"In the town of Bethlehem in Judaea", they answered. "For this is what the prophet wrote: 'Bethlehem in the land of Judah, you are by no means the least of the leading cities of Judah; for from you will come a leader who will guide my people Israel.'"

So Herod called the visitors from the east to a secret meeting and found out from them the exact time the star had appeared. Then he sent them to Bethlehem with these instructions: "Go and make a careful search for the child, and when you find him, let me know, so that I too may go and worship him."

And so they left, and on their way they saw the same star they had seen in the east. When they saw it, how happy they were, what joy was theirs! It went ahead of them until it stopped over the place where the child was. They went into the house, and when they saw the child with his mother Mary, they knelt down and worshipped him. They brought out their gifts of gold, frankincense and myrrh, and presented them to him.

Then they returned to their country by another road, since God had warned them in a dream not to go back to Herod.

Matthew 2. 1-12 (GNB)

415 *Wise men*

These are the things that make us wise:
— learning how our world works
— learning how to get on with other people . . .
Lord, make us wise today, tomorrow
and for the rest of our lives.

416 *Crowns*

You, Lord God, have crowned each of us with gifts:
'A' can sing; 'B' can jump;
'C' can count; 'D' can write.
We offer you the crowns you have given to us —
our gifts and our lives,
for you are our Lord and our God.

417 *Journeys*

Be with all those who are making journeys this day,
that they may find you, O Lord,
at their journey's end.

418 *Gold, frankincense and myrrh*

The most precious things we have are . . .
The most mysterious things we have are . . .
The most special things we have are . . .
We bring to you, O Lord, all that we have:
our hopes, our fears, our lives . . .
Accept our gifts
and fill our days with your beauty,
your glory
and your peace.

419 *Dreams*

Our dreams are often very strange.
We have had dreams of . . .
Lord, help us to understand ourselves
and to enjoy the life you have given to us.

420 *True wisdom*

O God, who by a star
didst guide the Wise Men to the worship of thy Son:
lead, we pray thee, to thyself
the wise and the great in every land,
that unto thee every knee may bow,
and every thought be brought into captivity;
through Jesus Christ our Lord.

> *The Book of Common Worship: Church of South India*

Lent

421 *The testing of Jesus*

Then the spirit led Jesus into the desert to be tempted by the Devil. After spending forty days and nights without food, Jesus was hungry. Then the Devil came to him and said, "If you are God's Son, order these stones to turn into bread."

But Jesus answered, "The scripture says, 'Man cannot live on bread alone, but needs every word that God speaks.'"

The the Devil took Jesus to Jerusalem, the Holy City, set him on the highest point of the Temple, and said to him, "If you are God's Son, throw yourself down, for the scripture says, 'God will give orders to his angels about you; they will hold you up with their hands, so that not even your feet will be hurt on the stones.'"

Jesus answered, "But the scripture also says, 'Do not put the Lord your God to the test.'"

Then the Devil took Jesus to a very high mountain and showed him all the kingdoms of the world in all their greatness. "All this I will give you," the Devil said, "if you kneel down and worship me."

Then Jesus answered, "Go away, Satan! The scripture says, "Worship the Lord your God and serve only him!'"

Then the Devil left Jesus; and angels came and helped him.

Matthew 4. 1-11 (GNB)

422 *Saying 'sorry'*

Dear God, we know that sometimes we do things
that hurt other people . . .
Please forgive us, for we are truly sorry.

423 *Ash Wednesday*

O God, we do not always do the right things.
We do not always tell the truth.
We do not always love people as we should . . .
but you forgive us
and then give us the strength
to become more like you want us to be . . .
thank you, God, for being God.

424 *Dark moments*

In the darkest moments of our lives, O God,
remind us that you are light,
that you are hope,
that you are love.

425 *Resolution*

Help us, dear God, to live with
thankful and generous hearts
this day and for evermore.

426 *The cross of ash*

As the ash is put upon our foreheads, O Lord,
we remember those things we have done
which are very wrong.
Please forgive us
and by your cross lead us from darkness into light,
this day and for evermore.

Mothering Sunday

427 *Mary, mother of Jesus*

In the sixth month of Elizabeth's pregnancy God sent the angel Gabriel to a town in Galilee named Nazareth. He had a message for a girl promised in marriage to a man named Joseph, who was a descendant of King David. The girl's name was Mary. The angel came to her and said, "Peace be with you! The Lord is with you and has greatly blessed you!"

Mary was deeply troubled by the angel's message, and she wondered what his words meant. The angel said to her, "Don't be afraid, Mary; God has been gracious to you. You will become pregnant and give birth to a son, and you will name him Jesus. He will be great and will be called the Son of the Most High God. The Lord God will make him a king, as his ancestor David was, and he will be the king of the descendants of Jacob for ever; his kingdom will never end!"

Mary said to the angel, "I am a virgin. How, then, can this be?"

The angel answered, "The Holy Spirit will come upon you, and God's power will rest upon you. For this reason the holy child will be called the Son of God. Remember your relative Elizabeth. It is said that she cannot have children, but she herself is now six months pregnant, even though she is very old. For there is nothing that God cannot do."

"I am the Lord's servant," said Mary; "may it happen to
me as you have said." And the angel left her.

Luke 1. 26-38 (GNB)

428 *Mothering Sunday*

God bless our mothers; we hold them up to you
that they may be blessed with your love,
your patience and your kindness
in all that they do, in all that they are.

429 *Fathers*

God bless our fathers; we hold them up to you
that they may be blessed with your love,
your patience and your kindness
in all that they do, in all that they are.

430 *People who look after us*

Father and Mother of us all,
thank you for those people who look after us;
may they care for us as you care for us —
with absolute love and trust and truth.

431 *Step-parents*

Lord God, when new people come to live in our home,
may they be patient and very, very kind
and think of us as well as themselves.

432 *Unhappy families*

O God, you are the only one we can turn to;
please, please bring kindness and peace back to our homes,
for we need you very much;
and help us to understand what is going on.

433 *Family life*

Father of all,
accept our thanks for the joys of family life.
Help us to live so that we may strengthen and enrich
the life of the family.
Help us to build with you
the kind of family which welcomes the stranger,
the lonely and the needy.
Teach us, through this small family,
to love the family of all mankind
and to realise our part in it.
In the name of Christ we ask this.

Brother John Charles, SSF

434 *Broken homes*

Father in heaven,
pattern of all parenthood and lover of children,
we pray for homes and families across the world*.
Sustain and comfort them in need and sorrow.
In times of bitterness, tension and division,
draw near to heal.

May parents and children together
be learners in the school of Christ,
daily increasing in mutual respect and understanding,
in tolerance and patience,
and in all-prevailing love;
through Jesus Christ our Lord.
or in this community   *Timothy Dudley-Smith*

435 *Mother Church*

Let your love so fill our church, O Lord,
that all who come to it
may be embraced by your power
and by your peace.

436 *Cathedrals*

In the soaring beauty of our cathedral, O God,
let your simple presence dwell,
that we may come close to you in holiness,
and in your holiness find our peace,
for Jesus' sake.

Palm Sunday

437 *Jesus enters Jerusalem*

Jesus said this and then went on to Jerusalem ahead of them. As he came near Bethphage and Bethany at the Mount of Olives, he sent two disciples ahead with these instructions: "Go to the village there ahead of you; as you go in, you will find a colt tied up that has never been ridden. Untie it and bring it here. If someone asks you why you are untying it, tell him that the Master needs it."

They went on their way and found everything just as Jesus had told them. As they were untying the colt, its owners said to them, "Why are you untying it?"

"The Master needs it," they answered, and they took the colt to Jesus. Then they threw their cloaks over the animal and helped Jesus get on. As he rode on, people spread their cloaks on the road.

When he came near Jerusalem, at the place where the road went down the Mount of Olives, the large crowd of his disciples began to thank God and praise him in loud voices for all the great things that they had seen: "God bless the king who comes in the name of the Lord! Peace in heaven and glory to God!"

Luke 19. 28-38 (GNB)

438 *Palm Sunday*

Hosanna! Hosanna! cried the crowds,
for they were very happy and excited . . .

Lord, help us to understand more of the life of Jesus
and to draw close to you —
when we are happy and when we are sad.

439 *Jesus as king*

O God, the father of us all,
on this day your Son was called a king;
let his life reign in our hearts,
that we may glorify you in all we think
and speak and do,
now and for ever.

440 *The triumphal entry*

Jesus, King of the universe,
ride on in humble majesty;
ride on through conflict and debate;
ride on through sweaty prayer and betrayal of friends;
ride on through mockery and unjust condemnation;
ride on through cruel suffering and ignoble death;
ride on to the empty tomb and your rising in triumph;
ride on to raise up your Church,
a new body for your service;
ride on, King Jesus,
to renew the whole earth in your image;
in compassion come to help us.

441 *Good times and bad times*

Lord Christ, your disciples followed you
with songs in their hearts,
but there were also times when they were tired,
times when they were afraid.
Be with us when we feel most exhausted,
that we may be nourished by your gentle peace.

442 *The servant king*

Father, may we learn the humility of Jesus
who became our king when he became our servant;
teach us how to serve others in his name and for his sake.

Maundy Thursday

443 *The Last Supper*

While they were eating, Jesus took a piece of bread, gave a prayer of thanks, broke it, and gave it to his disciples. "Take and eat it," he said; "this is my body."

Then he took a cup, gave thanks to God, and gave it to them. "Drink it, all of you," he said; "this is my blood, which seals God's covenant, my blood poured out for many for the forgiveness of sins. I tell you, I will never again drink this wine until the day I drink the new wine with you in my Father's Kingdom."

Then they sang a hymn and went out to the Mount of Olives.

Matthew 26. 26-30 (GNB)

444 *The gift of life*

Lord Jesus,
you gave your disciples the gift of your life
and made them very courageous;
may we accept your gift
and live our lives for your glory
with much thanksgiving.

445 *Invited to share in the supper*

God our Father,
you have invited us to share in the supper
which your Son gave to his Church
to proclaim his death until he comes.
May he nourish us by his presence,
and unite us in his love;
who is alive and reigns with you and the Holy Spirit,
one God now and for ever.

446 *Breaking bread*

Dear God,
wherever in the world people break bread together,
may they know the love of Jesus, your Son.

447 *Drinking wine*

Dear God,
wherever in the world people drink wine together,
may they know the forgiveness of Jesus, your Son.

448 *Serving others*

Lord, you have taught us
that we are to care for each other;
help us so to look after those in need
that we may all be healed
and know your refreshing love.

449 *Betrayal*

When your friends betrayed you, Lord,
you took their sin upon yourself
and forgave them.
Please forgive us when we betray those we love
and when we betray you,
for without your forgiveness
our lives will become bitter and sad.
We are sorry, O God.
O God, please forgive . . .

Good Friday

450 *Mockery and death*

The soldiers took Jesus inside to the courtyard of the governor's palace and called together the rest of the company. They put a purple robe on Jesus, made a crown out of thorny branches, and put it on his head. They they began to salute him: "Long live the King of the Jews!" They beat him over the head with a stick, spat on him, fell on their knees and bowed down to him. When they had finished mocking him, they took off the purple robe and put his own clothes back on him. Then they led him out to crucify him.

On the way they met a man named Simon, who was coming into the city from the country, and the soldiers forced him to carry Jesus' cross. (Simon was from Cirene and was the father of Alexander and Rufus.) They took Jesus to a place called Golgotha, which means "The Place of the Skull". There they tried to give him wine mixed with a drug called myrrh, but Jesus would not drink it. They crucified him and divided his clothes among themselves, throwing dice to see who would get which piece of clothing. It was nine o'clock in the morning when they crucified him. The notice of the accusation against him said: "The King of the Jews." They also crucified two bandits with Jesus, one on his right and the other on his left.

Mark 15. 16-28 (GNB)

451 *The crucifixion*

Lord Jesus,
you suffered so much pain and cruelty on the cross,
but through it all you held on to love.
Be with us whenever life is very, very tough
and keep us loving no matter what happens —
for that is your way —
the way that leads to peace and truth.

452 *The example of Jesus*

Blessed Lord,
you bore on the shameful cross an undeserved punishment,
and forgave even those who nailed you there.
You spoke comfort to those who were dying beside you,
even during your own agony.
Teach us your love and compassion.
We can only hope to follow your example if you guide us
every step of the way.

A.G. Bullivant

453 *Dying for love*

Help me today, Lord Jesus, to remember you
with all the love of my heart,
because you suffered and died on this day long ago.
Teach me to understand that you died for love,
that I may grow loving like you,
and be afraid of nothing but grieving God.

454 *Nothing conquers love*

On that Good Friday, Lord,
they tried everything.
They tried to quench your love with insults,
to drown your love in jeering,
to kill your love
by nailing you to a cross.
But your love was not to be beaten.
You forgave them their insults;
you forgave them the jeering;
you forgave them the piercing,
and in your forgiveness
your love conquered all
and rose into a new and everlasting life.

455 *Dying for sin*

Almighty God,
who gave your only Son to die for the sins of the world;
have mercy on all who are tempted
and on all who, through weakness or wilfulness,
fall into sin;
reveal to them your gracious love,
that turning to you for help,
they may be led into fellowship with you
and obedience to your will;
through Jesus Christ our Lord.

Easter Day

456 *The empty tomb*

Very early on the first day of the week, the women came to the tomb where Jesus' body was laid. They brought the spices they had prepared. They found that the stone had been rolled away from the entrance of the tomb. They went in, but they did not find the body of the Lord Jesus. While they were wondering about this, two men in shining clothes suddenly stood beside them. The women were very afraid; they bowed their heads to the ground. The men said to the women, "Why are you looking for a living person here? This is a place for the dead. Jesus is not here. He has risen from death! Do you remember what he said in Galilee? He said that the Son of Man must be given to evil men, be killed on a cross, and rise from death on the third day." Then the women remembered what Jesus had said.

The women left the tomb and told all these things to the eleven apostles and the other followers. These women were Mary Magdalene, Joanna, Mary the mother of James, and some other women. The women told the apostles everything that had happened at the tomb. But they did not believe the women. It sounded like nonsense. But Peter got up and ran to the tomb. He looked in, wondering about what had happened.

Luke 24. 1-12 (ICB)

457 *Easter Day*

Lord Jesus, Lord of the Dance,
you have broken the gates of death
and released us from its terrors;
spring up within our lives
that we may be your Easter people
and sing our 'Alleluias'
today, tomorrow and for ever.

458 *The footsteps of Christ*

Ah, the fragrance of new grass!
I hear His footsteps coming —
the Lord of the Resurrection!
   Jiro Sasaki, Bishop of Kyoto

459 *Mary Magdalen*

Risen Lord Jesus,
as Mary Magdalen met you in the garden
on the morning of your resurrection,
so may we meet you today and every day:
speak to us as you spoke to her;
reveal yourself as the living Lord;
renew our hope and kindle our joy,
and send us to share the good news with others.

460 *Living Christ*

Lord Jesus,
you are alive in our world:
alive in peals of laughter;
alive in the joy of love;
alive in the heart of music;
alive in the power of sunlight;
alive in the breath of life;
alive in the prayers
at the centre of our souls.
Lord Christ,
living Lord,
let us share in your most holy life
now and for ever.

461 *Risen Jesus*

Lord Jesus Christ,
risen from the tomb,
your love is let loose in the world;
let your love conquer my heart,
that I may become one of your disciples
and follow you for ever . . .

462 *'Supposing him to be the gardener'*

Often we don't recognise you, Lord,
even when you are very close;
open our eyes to see your love and power in the world.

463 *The light of Christ*

The light of Christ pierces the darkness
like a sword;
the light of Christ banishes the darkness
like a fire;
the light of Christ conquers the darkness
like a victorious army.
O light of Christ,
shine in our hearts and lives
and bring us your life and your eternal victory.

464 *Doubting Thomas*

Lord, keep us asking questions,
so that we may discover you —
in all we think and speak and do.

465 *'Peace be with you'*

You have promised your peace, O Lord —
so deep, deep inside our lives
let your peace flourish and grow.

466 *Easter gardens*

We have made an Easter garden . . .

Lord, deep in the centre of everything
there is your life, your energy, your love . . .
may we make room for you in our lives
that we may be beautiful for you.

467 *Easter eggs*

Lord, let the Easter eggs remind us always
that you have conquered death
and brought the promise of a new life
and a new spring to us all.

Ascension Day, Whitsun and Pentecost

468 *The new fire*

When the day of Pentecost came, all the believers were
gathered together in one place. Suddenly there was a noise
from the sky which sounded like a strong wind blowing,
and it filled the whole house where they were sitting. Then
they saw what looked like tongues of fire which spread out
and touched each person there. They were all filled with the
Holy Spirit and began to talk in other languages, as the
Spirit enabled them to speak.

Acts 2. 1-4 (GNB)

469 *Ascension Day*

Lord God,
you are the King of the Universe,
King of Creation,
and King of Glory.
We worship you on this kingly day.

470 *The Holy Spirit*

Lord, your life is let loose in your world,
making things new, bringing us peace, giving us hope.
We offer you our 'Hoorays' for your Holy Spirit . . .

471 *'Like a dove'*

A dove is white, pure . . .

Be gently around us like a cloud of white doves,
O Lord, our beautiful God.

472 *Tongues of fire*

Fire is red and burning and very powerful . . .

O God, warm our hearts and our lives
that we may radiate your love to the world for Jesus' sake.

473 *Understanding*

These are things we don't understand . . .

Lord, increase our understanding
of ourselves, of each other, of you,
through the power of your Holy Spirit.

Harvest

474 *The parable of the sower*

People kept coming to Jesus from one town after another;
and when a great crowd gathered, Jesus told this parable:
"Once there was a man who went out to sow corn. As
he scattered the seed in the field, some of it fell along the
path, where it was stepped on, and the birds ate it up. Some
of it fell on rocky ground, and when the plants sprouted,
they dried up because the soil had no moisture. Some of the
seed fell among thorn bushes, which grew up with the
plants and choked them. And some seeds fell in good soil;
the plants grew and produced corn, a hundred grains each."
And Jesus concluded, "Listen, then, if you have ears!"

Luke 8. 4-8 (GNB)

475 *The richness of the earth*

Heavenly Creator and Lord of the world,
you have given us the soil, in all its richness,
to be the source of our food.
Bless those who care for the earth,
that it may always be fruitful and good for our use.

476 *The sounds of a bakery*

For the soft soft murmur of flour:
    we thank you, O God.
For the shake and rattle of salt:
    we thank you, O God.
for the slap and bang of kneading dough:
    we thank you, O God.
For the 'oohs' and 'aahs' as we eat warm bread:
    we thank you, O God.

477 *The sounds of cooking and eating*

We love bacon sizzling:	"Sizzle, sizzle"
We love puddings steaming:	"Hiss, hiss"
We love toasters popping:	"Pop, pop"
We love pizzas grilling:	"Bubble, bubble"
For all the sounds	
that make our mouths water,	
Hooray to God:	"Hooray".

478 *Farmers*

Bless with your wisdom and patience, dear God,
the farmers of the world,
that they may work with you and your creation
for the good of us all.

479 *Aid organisers*

Father, take especial care
of people who give their talents to help the poor,
the starving and the homeless.
May we share the burden with them
and work always for the good of everyone everywhere.

480 *Moles*

Down in the ground the moles are burrowing,
laying their claim to the earth.
O God, help us to keep room in our world
for all your creatures,
and to rejoice in the unexpected.

481 *Swallows*

They've been gathering, wheeling and screaming
and soon they'll begin their huge journey south.

Lord, bless the swallows, the acrobats of summer,
and as we rejoice in their flight
keep us alert to the needs of those people
who will see them soon:
for we share your one world.

482 *Bulbs underground*

The bulbs are already sprouting roots
ready for the spring,
and the earth goes on its vast journey
of death and birth.
Open our eyes, dear Lord,
to the hidden forces of your creation
and to give you thanks,
simply because life *is*.

483 *Garden chair*

Lord, thank you for the pleasure of sitting and looking,
and being quiet and still.
Teach us to appreciate the peace of your world,
and may we have peace in our hearts.

484 *The harvest of all*

For the fruits of the earth: we thank you.
For the harvest of the sea: we thank you.
For the beauty of the sky: we thank you.
For your energy pulsing through the whole of creation:
we thank you, heavenly Father.

485 *Beautiful country*

Have you seen our country?
The meadows green with fresh spring grass,
the hedgerows murmuring with summer insects,
the mountains standing proud sentinels
about the jewelled lakes,
the forests whispering in an autumn breeze,
and flowers radiant with beauty . . .
You have given us a glorious country, O Lord,
help us to treat it with thankfulness
and gentle care,
for Jesus' sake.

All Saints and All Souls;
Light and Dark

486 *The light of the world*

Jesus spoke to the Pharisees again. "I am the light of the
world," he said. "Whoever follows me will have the light of
life and will never walk in darkness."

John 8. 12 (GNB)

487 *Lighting a candle*

"It's better to light a candle than curse the darkness . . ."
(Proverb)

So Lord,
help us to be creators of light and slayers of darkness
in all that we do.

488 *'Things that go bump in the night'*

Sometimes when we go to bed we think . . .
When we are frightening ourselves, dear God,
let us know that your love surrounds us and gives us peace.

489 *Light shining in darkness*

No matter what happens, dear God,
we know that your light is stronger than any darkness
and that you are always with us.
Thank you.

490 *Bonfires*

Just as the bonfire lights up the sky
and the sparks fly upwards,
so may our prayers, Lord,
giving glory to you
and comfort and joy to our friends.

491 *Dark places*

These are the places of which we are afraid:
a doorway,
a cupboard
an attic . . .

Lord, you are love.
Lord, you are peace.
Lord, you are our gentle strength
and you are with us wherever we go,
so we need not be afraid.

Famous Prayers

Famous Prayers

492

We beg you, Lord, to help and defend us.
Deliver the oppressed;
pity the insignificant;
raise the fallen;
show yourself to the needy;
heal the sick;
bring back those of your people who have gone astray;
feed the hungry;
lift up the weak;
take off the prisoner's chains.
May every nation come to know that you alone are God,
that Jesus Christ is your child,
that we are your people,
the sheep that you pasture.

St Clement of Rome (d. AD95)

493

God, the Father of our Lord Jesus Christ,
increase in us faith and truth and gentleness,
and grant us part and lot among his saints.

St Polycarp (69-155)

241

494

O Christ, Ruler and Lord of the world,
to thee we consecrate this land,
its sceptre and its power.
Guard thy land, guard it from every foe.

Emperor Constantine (272-337)

495

Almighty God, bestow upon us the meaning of words,
the light of understanding,
the nobility of diction
and the faith of the true nature.
And grant that what we believe, we may also speak.

St Hilary (315-67)

496

Almighty God, who hast given us grace at this time
with one accord to make our common supplications unto thee,
and dost promise,
that when two or three are gathered together in thy name,
thou wilt grant their requests;
fulfil now, O Lord, the desires and petitions of thy servants
as may be most expedient for them,
granting us in this world knowledge of thy truth,
and in the world to come life everlasting.

St Chrysostom (347-407)

497

Watch thou, O Lord,
with those who wake, or watch, or weep tonight,
and give thine angels charge over those who sleep.
Tend thy sick ones, O Lord Christ;
rest thy weary ones;
bless thy dying ones;
soothe thy suffering ones;
pity thine afflicted ones;
shield thy joyous ones,
and all for thy love's sake.

St Augustine (354-430)

498

I bind unto myself today
the power of God to hold and lead,
his eye to watch, his might to stay,
his ear to hearken to my need;
the wisdom of my God to teach,
his hand to guide, his shield to ward,
the word of God to give me speech,
his heavenly host to be my guard.

St Patrick (389-461)

499

O gracious and holy Father,
give us wisdom to perceive thee,
intelligence to understand thee,
diligence to seek thee,
patience to wait for thee,
eyes to behold thee,
a heart to meditate upon thee
and a life to proclaim thee;
through the power of the spirit of Jesus Christ our Lord.

Attributed to St Benedict (480-543)

500

Be thou a bright flame before me;
be thou a guiding star above me;
be thou a smooth path below me;
be thou a kindly shepherd behind me,
today, tonight and for ever.

St Columba (521-97)

501

O God, great and wonderful, who has created the heavens,
dwelling in the light and beauty thereof,
who has made the earth,
revealing thyself in every flower that opens;
let not mine eyes be blind to thee,
neither let mine heart be dead,
but teach me to praise thee,
even as the lark which offereth her song at daybreak.

St Isidore of Seville (560-636)

502

Christ is the morning star who,
when the darkness of the world is past,
brings to his saints
the promise of the light of life
and opens everlasting day.

Venerable Bede (673-735)

503

May the right hand of the Lord keep us ever in old age,
the grace of Christ continually defend us from the enemy.
O Lord, direct our hearts in the way of peace;
through Jesus Christ our Lord.

Bishop Aedelwald (8th century)

504

Eternal Light, shine into our hearts;
Eternal Goodness, deliver us from evil;
Eternal Power, be our support;
Eternal Wisdom, scatter the darkness of our ignorance;
Eternal Pity, have mercy on us,
that, with all our heart and mind and soul and strength,
we may seek thy face and be brought by thine infinite mercy
to thy holy presence;
through Jesus Christ our Lord.

Alcuin of York (735-804)

505

Lord God Almighty,
I pray thee for thy great mercy
and by the token of thy holy rood,
guide me to thy will, to my soul's need,
better than I can myself;
and shield me against my foes, seen and unseen;
and teach me to do thy will,
that I may inwardly love thee before all things
with a clean mind and a clean body.
For thou art my maker and my redeemer,
my help, my comfort, my trust, and my hope.
Praise and glory be to thee now, ever and ever,
world without end.

King Alfred (849-901)

506

O Lord our God,
grant us grace to desire thee with our whole heart,
so that, desiring thee,
we may seek and find thee;
and so finding thee, may love thee;
and loving thee may hate those sins
which separate us from thee,
for the sake of Jesus Christ.

St Anselm (1033-1109)

507

O Divine Master, grant that I may not so much seek
to be consoled as to console,
to be understood, as to understand,
to be loved, as to love,
for it is in giving that we receive,
it is in pardoning that we are pardoned,
and it is in dying that we are born
to eternal life.

St Francis of Assisi (1182-1226)

508

Lord, make me an instrument of thy peace;
where there is hatred, let me sow love;
where there is injury, pardon;
where there is discord, union;
where there is doubt, faith;
where there is despair, hope;
where there is darkness, light;
where there is sadness, joy;
for thy mercy's sake.
Attributed to St Francis of Assisi (1182-1226)

509

Thanks be to thee,
O Lord Jesus Christ,
For all the benefits
which thou hast won for us,
For all the pains and insults
which thou hast borne for us.
O most merciful Redeemer,
Friend and Brother,
may we know thee more clearly,
love thee more dearly,
and follow thee more nearly,
day by day.
St Richard of Chichester (1197-1253)

510

O Lord Jesus Christ, who created and redeemed me,
and hast brought me unto that which now I am,
thou knowest what thou wouldst do with me;
do with me according to thy will;
for thy tender mercy's sake.

King Henry VI (1421-1472)

511

O Lord Jesus Christ,
who art the way, the truth and the life;
we pray thee not to suffer us to stray from thee,
who art the way;
nor to distrust thee,
who art the truth;
nor to rest on any other than thee,
who art the life.
Teach us what to believe, what to do
and wherein to take our rest.

Erasmus (1467-1536)

512

Ah, dearest Jesus, holy Child,
make thee a bed, soft, undefiled
within my heart, that it may be
a quiet chamber kept for thee.

Martin Luther (1483-1546)

513

The things, good Lord, that we pray for,
give us grace to work for;
through Jesus Christ our Lord.

Thomas More (1478-1535)

514

O Lord our God,
give us by thy Holy Spirit
a willing heart and a ready hand
to use all thy gifts to thy praise and glory;
through Jesus Christ our Lord.

Archbishop Cranmer (1489-1556)

515

Teach us, good Lord, to serve thee as thou deservest.
To give and not to count the cost;
to fight and not to heed the wounds;
to toil and not to seek for rest;
to labour and not to ask for any reward
save that of knowing that we do thy will.

Ignatius Loyola (1491-1556)

516

O heavenly Father,
the Father of all wisdom, understanding and true strength,
send thy Holy Spirit into our hearts;
that when we must join the fight in the field
for the glory of thy holy name,
we may manfully stand strengthened by thee
in the confession of thy faith
and of thy truth to our life's end;
through Jesus Christ our Lord.

Bishop Nicholas Ridley (1500-1555)

517

Christ has no body now on earth but yours,
no hands but yours, no feet but yours;
yours are the eyes
 through which to look at Christ's compassion to the world,
yours are the feet
with which he is to go about doing good,
and yours are the hands
with which he is to bless us now.

St Teresa of Avila (1515-1582)

518

Lord God,
when you call your servants to endeavour any great matter,
grant us also to know that it is not the beginning,
but the continuing of the same,
until it be thoroughly finished,
which yields the true glory;
through him who, for the finishing of your work,
laid down his life for us,
our Redeemer, Jesus Christ.

Prayer based on the words of Sir Francis Drake

519

Give me my scallop-shell of quiet,
my staff of faith to walk upon,
my scrip of joy, immortal diet,
my bottle of salvation,
my gown of Glory, hope's true gage
and thus I'll take my pilgrimage.

Sir Walter Raleigh

520

Thou who hast given so much to me,
give one thing more,
a grateful heart,
for Christ's sake.

George Herbert (1593-1632)

521

Let all the world in every corner sing,
my God and King!
The heavens are not too high,
his praise may thither fly;
The earth is not too low,
his praises there may grow.
Let all the world in every corner sing,
my God and King!

George Herbert (1593-1632)

522

Bring us, O Lord God, at our last awakening
into the house and gate of heaven,
to enter into that gate and dwell in that house,
where there shall be no darkness nor dazzling,
but one equal light;
no noise nor silence,
but one equal music;
no fears nor hopes,
but one equal possession;
no ends, nor beginnings,
but one equal eternity;
in the habitations of thy glory and dominion,
world without end.

John Donne (1572-1631)

523

Let this day, O Lord,
add some knowledge or good deed to yesterday.

Lancelot Andrewes (1555-1626)

524

Open thou mine eyes, that I may see;
incline my heart, that I may desire;
order my steps, that I may follow
the way of thy commandments.

Lancelot Andrewes (1555-1626)

525

O Lord, thou knowest how busy I must be this day;
if I forget thee, do not thou forget me;
for Christ's sake.

General Lord Astley (1579-1652)
(before the battle of Edgehill)

526

Lord, let Thy glory be my end,
Thy word my rule,
and then Thy will be done.

King Charles I (1600-1648)

527

O Lord, baptise our hearts
into a sense of the conditions and needs of all men.

George Fox (1624-1691)

528

Lord, help me to know that:
he who is down need fear no fall,
he that is low, no pride;
he that is humble, ever shall
have God to be his guide.
Make me content with what I have,
little be it or much;
and, Lord, contentment ever crave,
because thou savest such.

Adapted from John Bunyan (1628-88)

529

Glory to thee, my God, this night,
for all the blessings of the light;
keep me, O keep me, King of Kings,
beneath thy own almighty wings.

Thomas Ken (1637-1711)

530

O God, help us not to despise or oppose
what we do not understand.

William Penn (1644-1718)

531

Bless me, O Lord,
and let my food strengthen me to serve thee,
for Jesus Christ's sake.

Isaac Watts (1674-1748)

532

O Lord, let us not live to be useless,
for Christ's sake.

John Wesley (1703-1791)

533

Make me remember, O God, that every day is your gift
and ought to be used according to thy command,
through Jesus Christ our Lord.

Samuel Johnson (1709-86)

534

He prayeth best, who loveth best,
all things both great and small;
for the dear God who loveth us,
he made and loveth all.

S T Coleridge (1772-1834)

535

Incline us, O God!
to think humbly of ourselves,
to be saved only in the examination of our own conduct,
to consider our fellow creatures with kindness,
and to judge of all they say and do
with the charity which we would desire from them ourselves.

Jane Austen (1775-1817)

536

Lord, we thy presence seek;
may ours this blessing be;
give us a pure and lowly heart
a temple meet for thee.

John Keble (1792-1866)

537

O Lord, support us all the day long of this troublous life,
until the shadows lengthen,
the evening comes,
the fever of life is over and our work on earth is done;
then Lord, in Thy mercy,
grant us safe lodging, a holy rest, and peace at the last.

Cardinal Newman (1801-90)

538

Drop thy still dews of quietness
till all our strivings cease;
take from our souls the strain and stress
and let our ordered lives confess
the beauty of Thy peace.

John Greenleaf Whittier (1807-92)

539

Guide us, teach us, and strengthen us, O Lord, we beseech thee,
until we become such as thou wouldst have us be,
pure, gentle, truthful,
high-minded, courteous, generous,
able, dutiful and useful;
for thy honour and glory.

Charles Kingsley (1819-1875)

540

Speak, Lord, for thy servant heareth.
Grant us ears to hear,
eyes to see,
wills to obey,
hearts to love,
then declare what thou wilt,
reveal what thou wilt,
command what thou wilt,
demand what thou wilt.

Christina Rossetti (1830-1894)

541

When the day returns,
call us with morning faces, and with morning hearts,
eager to labour,
happy if happiness be our portion,
and if the day is marked for sorrow,
strong to endure.

Robert Louis Stevenson (1850-1894)

542

Almighty God,
from whom all thoughts of truth and peace proceed;
kindle, we pray thee, in the hearts of all men
the true love of peace,
and guide with thy pure and peaceable wisdom
those who take counsel for the nations of the earth;
that in tranquillity thy kingdom may go forward,
till the earth be filled with the knowledge of thy love;
through Jesus Christ our Lord.

Bishop Francis Paget (1851-1911)

543

Here, Lord, is my life.
I place it on the altar today.
Use it as you will.
Albert Schweitzer (1875-1965)

544

O heavenly Father,
protect and bless all things that have breath:
guard them from all evil and let them sleep in peace.
Albert Schweitzer (1875-1967)

545

O God, our loving Father,
we pray thee to keep us ever close to thyself,
that we may find in thy love our strength and our peace.

Archbishop William Temple (1881-1944)

546

Night is drawing nigh —
for all that has been — Thanks!
To all that shall be — Yes!

Dag Hammarskjold (1905-1961)

547

God bless Africa.
Guard her children,
guide her rulers,
and give her peace,
for Jesus Christ's sake.

Bishop Trevor Huddleston

548

Make us worthy, Lord,
To serve our fellow-men throughout the world
who live and die in poverty or hunger.
Give them, through our hands, this day their daily bread,
and by our understanding love, give peace and joy.

Mother Teresa of Calcutta

549

Grant peace and eternal rest to all the departed,
but especially to the millions known and unknown
who died as prisoners in many lands,
victims of the hatred and cruelty of man.
May the example of their suffering and courage
draw us closer to thee through thine own agony and passion,
and thus strengthen us in our desire to serve thee
in the sick, the unwanted and the dying,
wherever we may find them.
Give us grace so to spend ourselves
for those who are still alive, that we may prove most truly
that we have not forgotten those who have died.

Sue Ryder and Leonard Cheshire

550

Our Father in heaven,
hallowed be your name,
your kingdom come,
your will be done,
on earth as in heaven.
Give us today our daily bread.
Forgive us our sins
as we forgive those
who sin against us.
Lead us not into temptation
but deliver us from evil.

For the kingdom, the power,
and the glory are yours
now and for ever. Amen.

Subject Index

Figures refer to individual prayers not pages

Author Index

Figures refer to individual prayers not pages

Scripture Index

Figures refer to individual prayers not pages

Acknowledgements

The compilation of this book would not have been possible without the dedicated assistance of my secretary Kathy Lilley and the exemplary help and encouragement of the editorial staff of the National Society.

The editor and publisher gratefully acknowledge permission to reproduce copyright material in this anthology. Every effort has been made to trace and contact copyright holders. If there are any inadvertent omissions we apologize to those concerned. Christopher Herbert has written, and retains the copyright of, all the prayers except those acknowledged in the main text or listed below.

Edward Arnold Publishers: from *Words for Worship* compiled by Christopher Campling and Michael Davis, 98, 105, 452. Augsburg Fortress: from *Lord I want to tell you something* by Chris Jones, 211. Central Board of Finance of the Church of England: from *The Promise of His Glory*, 384, 411, 413; from *Lent, Holy Week and Easter*, 445. Christian Aid: from *Caring for God's World* compiled by Geoffrey Hyder and Tony Hodgson, 155. Church Missionary Society: from *Morning, Noon and Night* compiled by John Carden, 28, 47, 142, 143, 160, 279, 420, 440, 458. Victor Gollancz: from *Prayers and Graces* by Allen Laing, 307. Hodder & Stoughton: from *Blessings* edited by Mary Craig, 549. Lutheran World Federation: from *Children in Conversation with God*, 15, 115, 138, 171. Lutterworth Press: from *Prayers at Breakfast* by Beryl Bye, 110, 111. Susan Mabe, 202. Mowbrays: from *Prayers for use at the Alternative Services* compiled by David Silk, 99, 156, 433, 434, 454. Oxford University Press: from *The Oxford Book of Prayer* edited by George Appleton, 74, 130, 547, 548; from *Prayer for Every Day* edited by Vicars Walker Bell, 104. Pan Macmillan: from *Prayers from the Ark* by Carmen Bernos de Gatzold, translated by Rumer Godden, 70, 71. Penguin Books: from *The Puffin Book of Prayers* compiled by Louis Carpenter, 21, 124, 125, 170, 194, 203, 220, 221, 259, 455. St. Andrew Press: from *Children Praying*, 385. St. Saviour's Priory, 292. SPCK: from *The Daily Office* by the Joint Liturgical Group, 91; from *The Hidden Garden of Prayer* by Edward Sedding, 278. Donald Swann, 187. USPG: from *The Oxford Book of Prayer* edited by George Appleton, 167.

Bible texts are used with permission from the *New English Bible* (NEB) © 1970 by permission of The Oxford and Cambridge University Presses; the *Good News Bible* (GNB) © American Bible Society, New York, 1966, 1971 and 4th edition 1976, published by The Bible Societies/HarperCollins; and the *International Children's Bible* (ICB) published by Word (UK).

Forward Movement Publications

Forward Movement Publications produces and distributes approximately two million copies of tracts, books and booklets each year. About half that total represents subscriptions to the quarterly devotional guide, *Forward Day by Day*. Forward Movement is a nonprofit publishing agency of the General Convention of the Episcopal Church. Since its establishment in 1934 its editorial and business offices have been located in Cincinnati.